The Poetic Imperative

The Poetic Imperative

A Speculative Aesthetics

JOHANNA SKIBSRUD

McGill-Queen's University Press
Montreal & Kingston • London • Chicago

ISBN 978-0-2280-0170-6 (cloth)
ISBN 978-0-2280-0305-2 (ePDF)
ISBN 978-0-2280-0306-9 (ePUB)

Legal deposit second quarter 2020
Bibliothèque nationale du Québec

Printed in Canada on acid-free paper that is 100% ancient forest free (100% post-consumer recycled), processed chlorine free

Funded by the Government of Canada | Financé par le gouvernement du Canada | Canada

Canada Council for the Arts | Conseil des arts du Canada

We acknowledge the support of the Canada Council for the Arts.
Nous remercions le Conseil des arts du Canada de son soutien.

Library and Archives Canada Cataloguing in Publication

Title: The poetic imperative : a speculative aesthetics / Johanna Skibsrud.
Names: Skibsrud, Johanna, 1980- author.
Description: Includes bibliographical references and index.
Identifiers: Canadiana (print) 20200155245 | Canadiana (ebook) 20200155288 | ISBN 9780228001706 (cloth) | ISBN 9780228003052 (ePDF) | ISBN 9780228003069 (ePUB)
Subjects: LCSH: Poetry, Modern—History and criticism. | LCSH: Poetics. | LCSH: Self in literature.
Classification: LCC PN1042.S62 2020 | DDC 809.1/03—dc23

For my mother, who first introduced me to poetry,
And taught me to read the world like a poem.

Contents

Acknowledgments • ix

Introduction • 3

1 "The Bees Come Booming": A Poetics of "As If" • 23

2 "One Kind of Knowledge": Poetry and Belief • 41

3 "Un coup de dés": The Secret History of Poetry – and Its Imaginary Future • 56

4 The Vanishing Point of Meaning: "Making Sense" of the Fugal Past • 79

5 "To Undo the Creature": The Paradox of Writing • 96

6 *Praxis* and *Poiesis*: The Subversive Structures of Poetry and Human Being • 119

7 The Future Library and the Xenotext: Poetry and the Futurism of the Present • 142

Notes • 155

References • 171

Index • 183

Acknowledgments

With heartfelt thanks to the people who made this book possible: the Social Sciences and Humanities Research Council; my mentors, Eric Savoy and Tenney Nathanson; my readers, Manya Lampert and Laura Berry; my editor, Mark Abley; my husband, John Melillo; and my mother, Janet Shively.

Excerpts from *It*, copyright ©1969, by Inger Christensen, translation copyright ©2005, 2006 by Susanna Nied, are reprinted by permission of New Directions Publishing Corp. All rights reserved.

Excerpts from "Mess Studies," appearing in *Mess and Mess and*, copyright ©2015, by Douglas Kearney, are reprinted by permission of Noemi Press. All rights reserved.

Excerpts from *O Cidadán*, copyright ©2008, by Erín Moure and *The Unmemntioable*, copyright ©2012, by Erín Moure, are reprinted by permission of House of Anansi Press. All rights reserved.

Excerpts from *Hacha*, copyright ©2008, by Craig Santos Perez, *Saina* copyright ©2010, by Craig Santos Perez, and *Guma* copyright ©2014, by Craig Santos Perez, are reprinted by permission of Omnidawn Publishing. All rights reserved.

Excerpts from the following pages: 6, 20, 102, 136, 191, 194–5, 197–8, 202, 204 from *Zong!*, copyright ©2007, by M. NourbeSe Philip, are reprinted by permission of Wesleyan University Press. All rights reserved.

Excerpts from "Poem out of Childhood," "In a Dark House," and "This Place in the Ways" appearing in *The Collected Poems of Muriel Rukeyser*, copyright ©2005, by Muriel Rukeyser, are reprinted by permission of ICM Partners. All rights reserved.

Excerpts from Angela Rawlings's *Áfall/Trauma* are reprinted by permission of the author. All rights reserved.

Excerpts from "Draft of a Voice-Over for Split-Screen Video Loop" appearing in *Magenta Soul Whip*, copyright ©2009, by Lisa Robertson, are reprinted by permission of Coach House Books. All rights reserved.

Excerpt from *Spit Temple*, by Cecilia Vicuña, translated by Rosa Alcalá, copyright ©2012, is reprinted by permission of Ugly Duckling Presse. All rights reserved.

The Poetic Imperative

Introduction

Prometheus stole fire. Pandora opened the box. Eve took a bite. Faust made a pact with the devil. Dr Frankenstein created a monster. The implication of bold defiance in all these acts is predicated on the sense of a natural limit to the category of the human – and the inherent danger of surpassing it. But what are the limits of the human, and how did they come to be defined? What does it mean to "know" those limits? What does it mean to reimagine or refuse them?

The earliest interpreters of the Delphic dictum "know thyself" construed it as counsel to know one's place – to recognize the limits of individual human knowledge and power.[1] But in the sixteenth century, "know thyself" began to suggest the wealth of scientific knowledge that could be gained by studying human anatomy through dissection. In 1735, at the height of the Enlightenment, the Swedish botanist Carl Linnaeus used a Latin translation of the phrase "nosce te ipsum" as the first taxonomic description of human being. Rather than – or as well as – a limit, the phrase now posed an intellectual and scientific challenge. It also laid the grounds for the paradoxical modern conception of human being as both "an object of knowledge and a subject that knows" (Foucault 1970, 312).[2]

This book is an effort at recouping the poetic imperative buried within the command to "know thyself." It approaches poetry and human being not as fixed categories but rather as active processes of self-reflection. Language and knowledge are not considered in their application *to* human being but instead as expressions of the way that human being is constantly being activated within and through language and knowledge. The poetic imperative to "know thyself" thus becomes a challenge to recognize subjective and material limits while leaving these borders undefined. It asks us to direct attention simultaneously to both the finite and embodied limits of selfhood, as well as to what those limits touch upon: the infinite, the Other, and truth itself.

In *Three Steps on the Ladder of Writing*, Hélène Cixous defines truth as "the thing you must not say": "The thing that is both known and unknown, the most unknown and the best unknown is what we are looking for when we write. We go toward the best thing, where knowing and not knowing touch, where we hope we will know what is unknown. Where we hope we will not be afraid of understanding the incomprehensible, facing the invisible, hearing the inaudible, thinking the unthinkable, which is of course: thinking. Thinking is trying to think the unthinkable" (1993, 38). Truth is understood here not as a totalizing abstraction but as a process of going "toward the best known thing, where knowing and not knowing touch." Truth – in other words – inheres in the proximity between "knowing and not knowing." It works at the unstable limits of subjectivity and knowledge, moving in the direction of what Virginia Woolf calls "the far side of language" (1925, 31).[3] Understood as an intimacy with strangeness and uncertainty, truth involves the interplay between conscious recognition and what cannot be either deciphered or named.

Knowledge is also involved in this interplay. It is produced not through a radical separation from what is unknown, but instead through active intuition involving the processes of touching and feeling. Poetry underscores this tangible and embodied aspect of knowledge – and, therefore, its relationship to Cixous's conception of truth. Through multivalent expressions of the sensual and impressionistic aspects of experience, poetry reveals knowledge not as a category exclusive to rational apprehension, but as a process of "perception, intuition, intimation" (OED 2018, 4d, 4e) evoking, and drawing upon, "personal acquaintance; friendship, intimacy" (OED 2018, 3b).

Poetry is not, therefore, only a literary form; it is also a commitment to encountering, and engaging with, what cannot finally be apprehended or articulated through rational thought and language. A fundamental connection to both myth and play[4] affords it the potential to pose essential questions without essentializing its position in relation to them or providing a ready response. It is *speculative* – departing from a point of conjecture and desire rather than from prior knowledge. As Allen Grossman concludes in the introductory note to *Summa Lyrica: A Primer of the Commonplaces in Speculative Poetics*, a poem is first and foremost a text "for use, intended ... to give rise to thoughts about something else" (1992, 208). A close relative to the riddle – one of the earliest recorded examples of speculative thought – poetry serves not as a repository of received knowledge, but rather as a playful disruption of sense and logic aimed at eliciting unexpected connections.

By examining a range of modern and contemporary poets engaged within this speculative tradition, my aim is to show that poetry extends beyond formal and generic categories toward the "unthinkable." In no way do I wish to undermine the reality and importance of poetry's aesthetic functions, the vital role of individual poems, or the validity of a historical approach to the poetic tradition as we currently understand it. I hope, instead, to emphasize poetry's inherent capacity to play with – and transgress – the boundaries of subject and object, known and unknown, mythic and real.

To a certain, inevitable extent, every poetic text operates by destabilizing symbolic representation, linear narrative, and "common sense" through its use of metaphor, enjambment, and lyric apostrophe.[5] The poetic projects I engage with in this study – though not united by a particular language, style, or approach – share a deep commitment to employing these basic poetic operatives as a means of self-reflexively addressing the limits of language and thought. Like many other poets working in a modernist or experimental tradition, the poets considered in these pages seek to consciously confront, and challenge, the limits and possibilities of their own form – as well as of their own time.

Eliot in "Tradition and the Individual Talent"[6] and Pound in his aphorism "literature is news that stays news" (1934, 29) describe poetry as always contemporary. A different kind of contemporaneity is explored by Jonathan Culler at the level of the text. He argues that lyric poetry is characterized by its performance of an event in "the special 'now'" afforded by apostrophic address (2015, 226). By establishing grounds for an event of speaking and listening that collapses the distance between subject and object and interrupts the progression of narrative time, poetry places us in "the continuing present … [where] for readers, a poetic event can repeatedly occur" (ibid.).

My focus will be on poets of the last century specifically interested in this fundamental or structural contemporaneity – as well as in the ways that contemporaneity at this level makes poetry particularly adept at expressing the urgencies and complexities of contemporary life. The modern and contemporary poets included in this book think and make poetry in a mode that self-consciously shows the poetic imperative "know thyself" at work both in and as the space of the poem. I hope to demonstrate this imperative as a command not only to speak and listen, but also as an urge to action and feeling. My broader aim is to expand our sense of the reach and potential impact of poetry by suggesting that the poetic imperative – though central and vital to poetry understood as a genre, or a collection of forms – is *also* at the root of any conscious effort to address oneself to the unknown.

Martin Heidegger defined the Greek origin of the word *poiesis* as the "bringing forth" or "presencing" of that which "is not yet" into what *is* (1977, 10). Giorgio Agamben puts it somewhat differently: *poiesis*, he writes, is the process by which something "passe[s] from nonbeing into being, thus opening a space of truth" (1999a, 70). Crucial to both definitions is an emphasis on the poetic project as revelation – on the disclosure, within a given structure, of something new. But as Heidegger's definition implies, poetry's generative – even prophetic – function is grounded in a self-reflexive awareness of its own limited form. By drawing attention to those limits, poetic texts offer ways of perceiving and expressing the immanence within what "is" of what is other, otherwise, or not yet – both spatially and temporally. As Fred Moten writes, poetry affords a "double-capacity to see the absolute brutality of the already-existing and to point it out and to tell that truth, but also to see the other way, to see what it could be" (2013, 131). I would add to this that poetry can also reveal that "the absolute brutality of the already existing" – what *is* – may not have been inevitable. Poetry disrupts the linear progression between past, present, and future, allowing us to glimpse the "un-inevitability" of every moment, and offering us a powerful and often painful reminder of our complicities within, as well as our vulnerabilities to, the political and historical forces that exceed us.

Although the poets I've included in this study are part of a long and complex tradition, an elaboration of which lies beyond the scope of this book, they each demonstrate a unique approach to the riddle of human being – and attempt to rewrite, from within, the rules of their own game. By looking at these poets together, I aim to challenge the polarized sense of poetry's role in our culture, entrenched at least since the Romantic era, as being either imitative of, or a deliberate departure from, lived reality.[7] Poetry, I argue, takes place in the intersections between these two categories. It is both creative and mimetic, "a way of happening" and a way of witnessing what happens.[8] Most importantly, it is a way of mirroring the self-reflexive, provisional, and speculative terrain of human being in order to remain undefined.[9]

The readings that follow are therefore of poets that move with intention through this uncertain terrain: they are poets who reveal poetry's amorphous borders as well as its mystifying contradictions – poets who, while pointing self-reflexively to the limits of their form, simultaneously attempt to move beyond them. Poetry, their work suggests, is a way of saying what we "must not" or "cannot" say (Cixous 1993, 36). It asks us to escape toward truth understood not as a form of personal expression, but as a movement beyond the finite and contingent sphere of the abstract subject. By simultaneously orienting itself toward what is "best known" (the self, the finite nearness of voice and subjectivity) and "what is unknown" (the distant, "far side" of subjectivity and language, which cannot be expressed in the "self-evident" or "given" sense of human being), poetic texts enact the paradox implicit within the imperative "know thyself" and question the boundaries between binary categories such as subject and object, human and non-human, life and death. In this way, poetry resists the totalizing impulses of (rational or irrational) scientific, philosophical, and critical discourses, as well as the dominant definitions of knowledge as "the action of acknowledging or owning something" or "the fact of recognizing someone or something already known" (OED 2018, 1a, 1b), elaborating instead a space of reflexivity and defamiliarization. The readings in this book describe how poetry arrives at process-based notions of truth and knowledge by expressing the always unequal relation between the sayable and what remains beyond both language and subjective understanding.

I begin with an examination of the role of the "as if" as a fundamentally speculative stance at the root of both the work of Wallace Stevens and the multidisciplinary artist Angela Rawlings. Of all the poets in this study, Stevens is one of the most canonical, and also perhaps the poet most conscious of himself *as* a poet. Working at the height of the modernist era, he spent his career attempting to redefine the possibilities and parameters of poetry while at the same time attempting to explode past the confines of language and every definition ("The poet is the priest of the invisible," he once wrote [1966, 908]; "The poem must resist the intelligence / Almost successfully" [1966, 306]; "It Must Be Abstract" [1966, 329]).

Like Stevens, Rawlings identifies as a poet and is interested in the speculative terrain opened up by poetic thinking: the way that attention to the processes of representation (what and how we see) can extend our thinking and experience. Rawlings's postmodern extension of her poetics – into the terrains of visual, sound, performance, and conceptual art – explicitly demonstrates that poetry must be understood as an approach to thinking and being rather than, or in addition to, being understood as a genre or form.

Chapter 2 turns to a consideration of the way in which the speculative approach to thinking and being described in Chapter 1 coalesces in approaches to knowledge and belief. The chapter focuses on the work of Muriel Rukeyser, who, with *The Book of the Dead*, innovated a fresh approach to the categories of both poetry and truth. Rukeyser prepared the way for a new generation of poets to poetically explore the limits and possibilities of documentation. Rather than avoiding, ignoring, or abstracting the world of facts, poetry, her work suggests, allows us to glimpse the ways in which facts arise as the result of complex and fluid processes of belief and knowledge. Poetry can therefore be a powerful way of expressing, and impelling us toward, our responsibility as witnesses to the world around us. We cannot change the facts as they currently exist, but we can, Rukeyser urges, change our relationship toward knowledge. By confronting the reality of what we *don't* know, as well as our complicity in defining the parameters of what counts as fact, we commit ourselves to a broadened conception of truth that cannot either be reduced to the "merely" apparent or used to support our own very particular version of things.[10]

Chapter 3 takes up and enacts the problems and possibilities of translation. It addresses the works of three very different poets: the French Symbolist poet Stéphane Mallarmé, whose "Un coup de dés" from 1897 shattered the definition of poetic form; the Danish poet Inger Christensen, whose innovative *It* [*Det*], first published in 1969, simultaneously addresses and complicates the boundaries between linguistic, political, and aesthetic categories, reinventing the poetic landscape; and the Chamorro poet Craig Santos Perez, whose *Unincorporated Territory* series (2008; 2010; 2014; 2017) provides a tangible expression of the intersections between different languages, histories, and identities. I argue that all three of these writers reveal poetry as a fundamentally plural and prophetic mode of production by resisting a conception of language and selfhood as isolated structures that might then be translated into other forms. By emphasizing language and selfhood as ongoing processes of translation, Mallarmé, Christensen, and Perez work to disrupt the notion of a linear progression between past, present, and future, and overturn the binary oppositions maintained by – and structurally necessary to – other forms of writing and knowledge.

Chapter 4 delves further into poetry's prophetic mode. I examine M. NourbeSe Philip's documentary poetic text *Zong!*, from 2002, and argue that poetry affords ways not only of describing or recounting historical events but of extending our perception of historical patterns and available forms.

Incorporating material from the infamous legal case *Gregson v. Gilbert* from 1783 – which followed the murder of roughly 150 slaves and the subsequent claim the owners of the slave ship *Zong* made against their insurers, seeking recompense for their lost "cargo" – Philip endeavours to tell an impossible story. She uses only the language made available by the sole surviving historical record of the *Zong* massacre, but by radically transforming it she gives voice to those whose lives the historical record systematically silenced and suppressed. Philip's poetic text – the subtitle of which reads, "As told to the author by Setaey Adamu Boateng" (the name Philip imagines for one of the murdered slaves) – is the author's effort to tell a "story that cannot be told, yet must be told" (2018, 198) and, as such, it provides an explicit example of the way that poetry can make present what is absent, or unnarratable – what exceeds subjectivity or refuses representation.

In Chapter 5 I further explore this poetic capacity to write past the borders of the subject though an analysis of the work of Anne Carson and an exploration of the concepts of "lack" and "desire." Although Carson emphasizes "lack" as a structural component within both language and being, I argue that it may be more apt to consider poetic texts and human subjectivity in terms of surplus and relation. As Carson's work demonstrates, it is not absence or lack that produces desire in poetry, but rather a recognition of the relation (the distance and, therefore, the potential proximity) between what can and can't be "told." Both explicitly and implicitly, Carson's work attests to the way in which attending to the limits or "edges" of both language and selfhood reveals both the problem of translation central to human experience and the possibility of communicating past it. Far from muteness, or incomprehension, what Carson's poetics – with its concern for distance and desire – ultimately demonstrates is the possibility of constantly reconfiguring the relation between telling and not telling, self and other.

Chapter 6 engages this argument within a larger discussion of poetry as an expression of the elliptical relation between *praxis* and *poiesis*. Through close readings of the work of three contemporary poets – Erín Moure, Lisa Robertson, and Douglas Kearney – I propose that rather than an art of imitation (as Aristotle maintains in his *Poetics*), poetry is the expression of the ambiguous territory between making and doing at the heart of every human action. As the work of Moure and Robertson shows, this effort often involves attention to the limits of both expression and comprehension. Both poets demonstrate the difficulty of translating words into meaning, meaning into action, but they do so in order to emphasize the contiguities between "inner" processes like identity formation and abstract thinking and their external manifestations.

Douglas Kearney's physical performances enact this ambiguous terrain between making and doing even more explicitly. Like Walter Benjamin's description of Paul Klee's "Angel of History," Kearney's performances evoke history not as a narrative mode but as a poetic *act* – a "state of emergency" that, without denying or abstracting from material and embodied reality, affords the possibility of new expressions of subjectivity. Kearney demonstrates that attending to the poetic imperative "know thyself" is possible only by acknowledging the limits of language, of subjectivity, of the body, and of knowing at all. His performances invite audiences to meet him at the "edge" of all four of these categories and, thereby, to confront the limitations of our thinking and our identities – as well as the possibility of moving past them.

This book is a celebration of poetry's capacity to conceive, in this way, of a movement beyond the limits of language and the finite subject – but it also recognizes the risks inherent both to identifying these limits and presuming to speaking past them. In the book's final chapter, I endeavour to address these risks through a discussion of two different conceptual projects: Katie Paterson's *The Future Library* and Christian Bök's *The Xenotext Experiment*. I argue that the movement these different projects describe – between subjects and objects as well as between finite and infinite timescales – valuably expands our concept of human being beyond the isolated figure of the abstract subject and encourages an enlarged sense of our responsibilities *as* human beings within this broadened context of both space and time. I also argue, however, that willfully overlooking the partial nature of all forms of human exploration and discourse, and the fundamentally relative nature of perception and scale, risks re-inscribing the limits of subjectivity and language by projecting a specific point of view as a universal truth. Poetry, I contend, offers us a way of moving simultaneously in two directions – on the one hand toward a recognition of subjective limits and, on the other hand, past them. It allows us the opportunity to both expand our concept of what it means to be human beyond the limits of selfhood *and* to acknowledge the partiality – as well as the unique value – of a particular point of view.

In this book, I will be concentrating on writers and artists who consciously identify as poets who write poetry. My hope, however, is that my readings of their work will direct us toward a broader understanding of what poetry is and how it functions beyond the generic category of "poetry" and the bounds of particular poems. By beginning and ending with considerations of multi-media artists – Katie Paterson and Angela Rawlings – I provide explicit examples of "the poetic" at work within non-linguistic materials. Through an emphasis on the limits and possibilities of communication and translation over vast distances and periods of time, both Rawlings and Paterson demonstrate not only that the semiotic realm extends well beyond specifically language-based art and thinking, but also that the poetic imperative extends well beyond the material product of a poem.

As evidenced by this comparative approach to twentieth- and twenty-first-century poets and artists, poetic texts are often deeply connected to an acknowledgement of their own limited forms. It is, indeed, through a commitment to their own partiality that they move specifically away from the idea of an "end" in transparent communication and toward the proliferation of multiple possible meanings. And yet this centrifugal, multivalent trajectory is not wholly distinct from the Symbolist desire for wholeness, perfection, and the absolute that I refer to in chapter 3 through a consideration of the work of Stéphane Mallarmé. In fact, I see Mallarmé's deliberate, even exaggerated, effort to direct his creative work past the limits of both the subject and of poetic form as a striking illustration of the poetic imperative this project sets out to explore. My hope is that the poetry taken up in this study can be understood to exist as part of a constellation of poetic texts that includes Mallarmé's groundbreaking "Un coup de dés."

One of the primary aims of this book is to show that the extraordinary ambition and presumptuous desire that shaped Mallarmé's work should not be considered separately from the goals that continue to guide the "postmodern" poetry of today. The commitment to fragmentation, hybridity, and to the expression of the limitations of language and subjectivity shared by so many twentieth and twenty-first century poets need not, that is, be understood as a rejection of symbolic categories such as "truth" and "meaning." Instead, these preoccupations demonstrate a continued commitment to confronting the role that the partial, the paradoxical, the illusive, and the imaginary play in creating the truth about our histories, politics, and everyday lives.

"It may be only a chimera," Mallarmé wrote of "the pure work" he hoped to achieve one day, "but merely to have thought of it attests … how much the present cycle, or the final quarter-century, has been struck by some absolute illumination" (2007, 209). Mallarmé recognizes that what he is seeking may (possibly) be only a "chimera," but he refuses to concede either the real, effective power that chimera has in the world or its confirmation of "absolute illumination." It is this capacity to recognize what (may be) illusory or imaginary as nonetheless integral to thought and experience that, I argue, continues to define the unique relationship poetry maintains between potentiality and actuality, the unknown and the known.

By punctuating this study with a discussion of poetry in translation in chapter 3, my goal is to underline this unique relationship – and point to poetry's very real facility in moving beyond the event of the "original" text. I consider the translated texts of Stéphane Mallarmé and Inger Christensen alongside the polysemic poetics of Craig Santos Perez in order to highlight poetry as an exploration and enactment of the process of translation itself. Like J.L. Austin's examples of performative speech acts (uttering "I do" in the exchange of marriage vows or challenging a friend "I bet you sixpence it will rain"), I argue that a poem is an active doing rather than a formal object (a description *of* doing, or a statement of the fact that something has been done) and that – because of this – the emphasis within poetic speech is not on the strict verifiability of any statement a poem might make, or on the possibility of being "accurately" interpreted. Instead, a poem's truth value must be understood to both include and *exceed* the possibility of being construed as either verifiably true or false. Even poetry that functions at a social level – documentary poetry, for example, in the case of Perez – includes the intuitive, associative, and performative aspects of human experience in conjunction with facts, testimony, and description.

In other words, poetry is never separate from, let alone "superior" to,[11] other modes of discourse – but neither is it simply a more self-reflexive way of "produc(ing) a systematic knowledge and accurate understanding of what it discusses" (Easthope 2013, 18). Instead, poetry works against discourse (understood as either unconscious or conscious manifestations of "systematic knowledge") by rendering discourse legible *as* discourse – as a system that can be engaged with and/or refused, resisted and/or redefined.

It is not surprising, then, that poetry tends to have a difficult, even unhappy, relationship to its own possibilities and form. The sheer number of times that poets have felt the need to come to poetry's "defense"[12] is testament to this, as is the number of poets who have given poetry up – despairing of its capacity to transcend the limits of material and / or subjective discourse. In the third century BCE, Plato barred poets from his imaginary republic for failing to directly represent reality. Over two thousand years later, Coleridge effected a reversal of this ban: by unequivocally equating poetry with truth, but strongly doubting his own ability to express it, Coleridge effectively self-censured his poetic output.

In the twentieth century, George Oppen famously fell "silent" for a period of nearly twenty years due to his conviction that poetry would never be able to properly speak to, let alone lessen or alleviate, human suffering. Theodor Adorno declared that "to write poetry after Auschwitz is barbaric" (1983, 34). Laura Riding permanently renounced the form because of the breach she perceived between poetry's "creed" and its "craft," which – she believed – made it ultimately irreconcilable with truth (Fisher 2010, 1).[13]

Marianne Moore's "I, too, dislike it"[14] may, however, still be the best known contemporary example of the ironic distance even the most devoted poets, and lovers of poetry, maintain between themselves and their form. In a recent essay titled (in tribute to Moore) "The Hatred of Poetry," Ben Lerner explains this distance by stating simply "poetry is a word for a kind of value no particular poem can realize" (2016, 53). By concentrating on the schism between the pure possibility of poetic expression and the limitations of actual poems, such a definition ends up undermining the real and continuous relationship that exists between desire and realizable form. This book argues that it is in fact poetry's *apparent* "unrealizability" that constitutes its actual and potential value. It proposes that poems *don't* fail, but operate by exposing the limits of subjectivity, language, and the present moment to chance and play – and by revealing this uncertain terrain as the territory of human being itself.[15]

There is no doubt, however, that poetry's relatively minor role within popular culture in the West, as well as the fear or "hatred" of poetry expressed even by its devotees, can be understood as a result of this complicity with, and revelation of, the uncertainty at the heart of thought and what it means to be human. Plato's famous prohibition of poets from his utopian Republic is both an expression of the difficult relationship that persists between poetry and the polis and a testament to poetry's fundamentally subversive nature – its capacity to disrupt meaning, dissolve difference, and overturn fixed categories.

As we learned from *The Republic*, poetry is not about poems: it is about "feed[ing] and water[ing] the passions instead of drying them up" (Plato 1888, 322); it is about reimagining history, lived experience, and the "useful" lies of a well-ordered state (Plato 1888, 72). Through poetry – as the poets included in this study show – the limits of the individual and the limits of the political are confronted both to call these categories into question and to create contact with what exists, unthinkably, beyond them. By rendering legible the inherent vulnerability of language, identity, and a linear conception of time to what exceeds or undoes these (and other) attempts at naming and knowing, their work offers us a way of recognizing ourselves within, and as, the fundamental riddle – "know thyself" – of human being. While playfully disrupting sense and actively resisting ready meaning, their work also manages to urgently convey that "something is at stake" (Huizinga 2014, 49)[16] in the poem – and that by acknowledging this we acknowledge a valuable, and sustainable, resource. "Everywhere we are told," Muriel Rukeyser once wrote: "that our human resources are all *to be used*, that our civilization itself means the uses of everything it has – the inventions, the histories, every scrap of fact. But there is one kind of knowledge – infinitely precious, time-resistant more than monuments, here to be passed between the generations in any way it may be: never to be used. And that is poetry" (120–1).

This book endeavours to recognize and harness the powerful resource we have in poetry while resisting, as much as possible, the grammar and political economy of "use." Because of its integral connection to other discourses, its capacity to both define and initiate points of contact between many different identities, and its power to bolster resistance and influence social movements,[17] poetry – I argue – is not a product or expression of a given culture's ethics or aesthetics. It is, instead, the very grounds of their making.

1 "The Bees Come Booming"
A Poetics of "As If"

In Wallace Stevens's long poem from 1942 "Notes toward a Supreme Fiction," he writes: "The bees come booming / As if – The pigeons clatter in the air" (1966, 337). Rather than directing us toward an immediate apperception of an image or idea, Stevens's "as if" – left dangling in this line, purposely unresolved – instead points to the "totality of involvements" the act of seeing, and interpreting, is more likely to hide (Heidegger 1962, 189).

Stevens's interest in this poem and throughout his career was in exploring language not as a means to merely describe experience but as the material foundation for interpretive possibility. Charles Altieri usefully compares this "concern for possibility" in Stevens's work to Martin Heidegger's approach to interpretation in *Being and Time*, referring to their shared "grammar of as" (2013, 241). As the line above makes clear, however, Stevens's interest was specifically in extending language beyond the "totality" implicated by subjective perception toward a more inclusive – if more uncertain – sense of the "total" or "real." Where – that is – the "as-structure" Heidegger identifies for interpretation and understanding is specifically delimited to what the perceiving subject already knows, Stevens's "concern for possibility" is for possibility *par excellence*: a field of immanent and potential relationality that extends beyond prior knowledge and understanding and is best expressed not through a discourse of potential equivalence and use (a grammar of "as") but of inequivalence (a grammar of "as if").[1]

Poetry, Stevens's oeuvre suggests to us, finally, is not just a literary form; it is instead an approach to thought and to being that uncovers the ultimate *inequivalence* between subjective identity and the objective, non-human world. Poetry moves us – as Stevens writes in "Notes" – toward "greater aptitude and apprehension" (1966, 334), an enlarged scope made possible through attention both to the immediacy of sensible perception and to the distance afforded by the speculative imagination. When, for example, in the same poem, the immersive, sensible quality – rather than merely the abstract concept – of "lounging by the sea" is transferred to the reader, an apprehension of a "totality" that simultaneously includes and radically excludes an individual point of view may be the result. The image of waves beating on the shore comes to exist not "as" a specific entity in relation to subjective understanding, but instead as a greater imaginative experience stemming from an awareness of the limits of both experience and its expression. Extending his poetic image past the "as-structure" of direct representation and interpretation, Stevens reveals a more expansive possibility. For both speaker and reader, at this point in the poem, it becomes, suddenly: "*As if* the waves at last were never broken / *As if* the language, suddenly, with ease / Said things it had laboriously spoken" (Stevens 1966, 334, emphasis added).

As suggested through this passage, poetry affords a way of accessing language beyond the "laboriously spoken" by inviting the reader to exist, like a poetic subject, not "as" but "as if" human. To exist in this way is to recognize the difference as well as the relation between language and the world to which it refers – between the "supreme fiction" of imagination and perception and the incontrovertible fact of being.

When we see a raven on the lawn, or a rose in a vase, we do not necessarily think "What is a raven?" or "What is meant by a rose?" in the way that we do when a raven or a rose enters a poem. Through metaphor, apostrophic address and word play, poetry emphasizes the inherently "fictive" nature of both language and perception, while at the same time pointing us, like a mathematical equation, toward multiple interpretive possibilities beyond its limited symbolic form.

Unlike mathematics, however, poetry fails to conceive of (let alone embody) a solution to its problems. Stevens's decision not to resolve his "As if – " in a metaphor that might satisfy a reader's desire for a meaningful sense of the "total" or whole makes this almost painfully clear – as does, in a very different way, Stevens's "The Motive for Metaphor," which strives neither to *arrive* at the "vital, arrogant, fatal dominant X" (1966, 257) it presents, nor to hide it. In this poem, "X" seems to mark the spot of direct, unmediated experience, but rather than acting as a singular, withheld solution to the poem, it directs us toward the poetic imperative both to acknowledge subjective and linguistic limits and to stride past them – extending both language and thought beyond readily available concepts or forms.

It is neither "reality," therefore, nor "imagination," neither "fact" nor "fiction" that is truly "supreme" for Stevens. Instead, it is metaphor – the "motive" of which is to present the rift between finite perception and the world beyond *not* as a stopping-point but as a space of speculative interpretation. What is meaningful, after all, Stevens suggests, at least in a poetic sense, is not a description or even necessarily an experience of what *is*, but the relation between what *is* and what is merely possible, or potential – what remains half-hidden, or in-between.

"You like it under the trees in autumn," Stevens writes, "Because everything is half-dead ... "

> In the same way, you were happy in spring,
> With half colors of quarter-things,
> The slightly brighter sky, the melting clouds,
> The single bird, the obscure moon. (1966, 257)

We are "happy," Stevens implies here, only when afforded the freedom to revitalize the objective content of experience through imaginative interpretation. And yet, this interpretive process also threatens to intrude upon, cover over, and even inhibit our immediate encounters with the world around us.

As the poem continues, we see how the "happy" elements of experience seem to dissolve under the scrutiny of attention and their expression through language: "The obscure moon lighting an obscure world / Of things that would never be quite expressed, / Where you yourself were never quite yourself / And did not want nor have to be" (1966, 257). Like the already refracted, "obscure" moonlight that illuminates an "obscure" world, the subject of this poem can be understood only in relation to what exceeds or refuses subjectivity. To deny this mediated aspect of experience, the poem suggests, would be to deny the way that subjective experience is constituted. The poem provides a means of highlighting the necessary but always inequivalent relation between what exists as fact – beyond the subject's individual perception and experience – and what exists, or is brought about, through the subject's refracted relation to the objective world and the very fact of being.

In Stevens's "Ordinary Evening in New Haven," for example, we can see that the perception of natural objects – such as an experience of the "fans and fragrance" of pine trees – emerges only because those objects (and thus every experience of them) have been "staked solidly in a gusty grappling with rocks" (1966, 416). Abstract expressions of experience are arrived at not through the superimposition of rational or nonfigurative concepts but instead by laying bare the physical or material structures from which sensible experiences arise. "The glass of the air becomes an element," Stevens continues:

> It was something imagined that has been washed away.
> A clearness has returned. It stands restored.
>
> It is not an empty clearness, a bottomless sight.
> It is a visibility of thought,
> In which hundreds of eyes, in one mind, see at once.
> (1966, 416)

Stevens's aim here is to articulate the relation between the limits of subjective perception and the "greater aptitude and apprehension" (Stevens 1966, 334) made available through poetry. The "hundreds of eyes, in one mind, [that] see at once" represent not, that is, "a bottomless sight" that can be imagined as having finally, and singly, transcended the material structures of language and subjectivity, but instead the poetic possibility of simultaneously perceiving multiple different perspectives and interpretations.

Stevens brings the generative significance of the literal and the material into still sharper focus through his emphasis on the graphic elements of the language he employs. From *Harmonium*'s straightforward symbolic substitution of the unknown with the letter X ("Huge are the canna in the dreams of / X, the mighty thought, the mighty man") to the interruptive null point introduced by "the never-rounding O" in "Montrechet-le-Jardin," to the "vital, arrogant, fatal dominant X" (1966, 257) that governs "The Motive for Metaphor," Stevens emphasizes the symbolic dimension of language more often hidden within apparent meaning. By revealing language as zero-degree code standing in for some other unknown referent, Stevens draws attention to the way that meaning is created through the tension – immanent within every instance of language – between the opacity of a text and imaginative possibility. Language, for Stevens, is – in other words – *poiesis,* a term that, in "Large Red Man Reading," he defines by referring, significantly, both to "literal characters" and "vatic lines": "The outlines of being and its expressings, the syllables of its law: / *Poesis, poesis,* the literal characters, the vatic lines" (1966, 365).

Poetry doesn't *transcend* the fact of its inscription on the page, this poem suggests; instead, it is constituted through the relation between "literal characters" and the ongoing interpretive possibilities presented by their encounter on the page. It is both material and prophetic, representing the substantial "fact" of language and its history (including established conceptual frameworks) and projected, future interpretations. It is "fictional" – but supremely so, and not in the pragmatic sense suggested by Hans Vaihinger's influential 1911 treatise, *The Philosophy of 'As If': A System of the Theoretical, Practical and Religious Fictions of Mankind.*

Vaihinger's dual assumptions that all of our systems of knowledge are essentially fictional and that the world of ideas is dedicated not to "the portrayal of reality" but to "finding our way about more easily in this world" (1935, 15) were influential to Stevens.[2] And yet Stevens's poetry questions –

rather than systematically supports – the narrative and pragmatic fictions of our lived realities. Poetry might indeed "help people live their lives," as he suggests in his essay "The Necessary Angel" from 1951 (1966, 621), but rather than reflecting Vaihinger's pragmatic estimation of the value of the imagination – its capacity to *hide* difference, in order that we might find our way "more easily in this world" – Stevens highlights the imaginative possibilities that become available only by confronting the essential difference between subjective and objective realities, and accepting the essential difficulty of navigating that distance.

The "vital X" tips toward meaning without ever offering, or even suggesting, the possibility of an ultimate solution; the bees come booming not with one but with every conceivable relation. Poetry orients itself past the limits of what can be definitively named – or what can be usefully employed. It moves – as Hélène Cixous has observed – toward truth and death (1993, 36): "Telling the truth and dying go together … our lives are buildings made out of lies. We have to lie to live" (1993, 36). Though seemingly in agreement with Vaihinger's basic premise that human experience and every system of knowledge is essentially fictional, Cixous does not view such "fictionalism" as a pragmatic and necessary choice to be embraced but instead suggests that literary writing can be a way of "unlying."[3] Literary writing – poetic writing – moves specifically away from the descriptive and expository properties of language and, therefore, of singular meaning. To "unlie" is not to supplant one definitive statement with another but instead to extend the specific syntax employed by a text toward the unknown.

Rather than a category or limit of knowledge, this hypothetical terrain – outside of, but still relative to, both subject and text – should be understood as an active process that does not end at the borders of the subject. The "as if-structure" of poetic texts takes an imaginative leap beyond the more immediate "as-structure" of hermeneutic understanding, impelling readers to attend both to difference and to the possibility (despite or because of difference) of contact and exchange. It induces a confrontation with what interrupts subjective perspective, thought, and language, and through that confrontation reveals finally not an impasse for language and thought, but a space of what we might call, after Maurice Blanchot, "infinite conversation."[4]

The ethical implications of this poetic orientation past the boundaries of the subject are made acutely apparent by the contemporary poet and interdisciplinary artist Angela Rawlings. Rawlings advocates for a broader, and more literal, understanding of what it might mean to address – even to "converse" with – the natural or non-human world through her essays, plays, poems, digital work, and photography. In an essay titled "Ecolinguistic Activism and How to Rite," she urges us to reframe our understanding of landscapes from "a use-value position" to an inclusive and immersive position "of ecocentric egalitarianism where humans, non-human entities, and ecosystems and their components are capable of communicating through multiple senses," and argues that "to hold a conversation with a landscape and its non-human inhabitants could cause a transition from metaphor to reality" (2015, 268).

This suggestion is itself carried over from metaphor to reality as Rawlings physically traverses glacial sites, engages with the landscape, and presents us with the artefacts of that engagement through images, sound archives, and text. Where Stevens, that is, represented the absolute beyond of human being through metaphoric figures like his famous "Snow Man," Rawlings renders the metaphor literal through a series of encounters with glacial ice. Her "conversations" with glaciers and other non-human entities serve to reframe the relationship between subject and object, human and non-human, what can and cannot be addressed: "Like landscapes, are our own bodily borders unnecessarily inhibiting our abilities to identify our interconnections? Are we not also water, contributing through in-flows and out-flows to other systems, or actively a part of these systems?" (2015, 279). What Stevens conceived of as poetry's "supreme fiction" Rawlings conceives as a way of moving toward "authenticity." "We frame experience in shorthand narratives because it is impossible to relate and represent an experience within the same parameters in which it originally occurred," she explains in an interview (2018, np). To confront the impossibility of a direct, unmediated representation of lived experience is also to confront the tremendous responsibility we have as interpreters of experience. "I grapple with my compulsion for authenticity," writes Rawlings, "towards a real connection, a material being-with, whether it is a being with self or with other bodies" (2018, np). Like Stevens, Rawlings provokes a sense of proximity and imaginative contact between representational language and selfhood and the absolutely unrepresentable in order to arrive at a sense of "real connection" between lived experience and its account.

Within "The Snow Man," Stevens deliberately builds tension between the forms of nothing perceived by the titular subject and their literal rendering on the page until, in the poem's final line, we arrive at an "impossible" presentation of the gap between subjectivity and objectivity in the form of "the nothing that is not there and the nothing that is" (1966, 8). It is into the space of this gap between two different kinds of nothing (nothing as absence in the form of "Nothing that is not there" and nothing as presence in the form of "the nothing that is") that Stevens playfully invites his readers to confront, and momentarily to overstep, the bounds of selfhood, language, and human existence itself. Rawlings similarly invites her readers to "think the unthinkable" (1993, 38) through the representation of her personal encounters with glacial landscapes. Having visited a range of different sites, from "melting glacial tongues and freshly exposed moraine to flooding glacial river and glacial peak," Rawlings writes: "These locales provided me with a unique opportunity to witness, document, and interact with nonhuman entities over a period of time and within a variety of roles ranging from tourist and artist to listener and, finally, cancer patient" (2015, 269).

For both poets, ice provides a metaphor for, and a site of engagement with, the limits and possibilities of language and perception because of its ambiguous relation to material definition. Recognizing ice as the solid and static articulation of what is also (either potentially or otherwise) liquid and flowing, both Stevens and Rawlings employ the ice object in their work to suggest the possibility of contact and interface between subject and object, linguistic and non-linguistic, life and death. Stevens displaces human subjectivity by locating both the subject and object of "The Snow Man" within a literal "mind of winter" and, in doing so, arrives at a conceptual encounter with what negates or refuses the inherent "fictionalism" of our structures of language, selfhood, and knowledge. Rawlings juxtaposes her own transforming body with the transforming landscape of Icelandic glaciers in order, as she puts it, to "reflect the other, be in relation to the other" (2015, 279) and reimagine real possibilities for human–non-human relationships that would go beyond the presumed potential "use value" of the latter.

For both, the metaphor of ice (and metaphor more generally) is employed not to suggest an abstract category of meaning, but the potential within both language and subjectivity for reflection and refraction. Like ice, both language and subjectivity can be conceived of as definite (described by a fixed and limited structure) and indefinite (fluid and ever-changing, offering countless opportunities for engagement and reinterpretation). By directing our attention to the definite (fixed and limited) structures of language, body, and subjective perception, both Stevens and Rawlings reveal the indefinite potential – immanent within every finite structure – for infinite possible relation.

Rawlings uses ritual, personal experience, and a practical pedagogy that involves soundwalks (the practice of active listening) in order to draw attention to the distance, as well as to the possibility of relation, between herself and the landscape around her. In anticipation of a round of chemotherapy, for example, Rawlings cut off her long hair beneath the Snæfellsjökull glacier (2015, 274). Four months after her mastectomy she walked bare-chested toward Svínafellsjökull glacier while the snow fell (2015, 276). A month later, she photographed trash in the Snæfellsjökull region, "searching for [her] excised breast" (2015, 276).

Rawlings's goal for these "conversations" with the landscape around her is that they remain open – an approach that is mirrored by the creative productions that grew out of them. Of a play titled *Áfall / Trauma*, Rawlings writes, it "functions as lived performance, with scripts designed for expansive interpretive flexibility" (2015, 272). The experience of reading or viewing *Áfall / Trauma* is purposely disorienting. Icelandic words, left untranslated, engage Rawlings's primarily English-speaking audience in "the experience of situational dysfluency, unanticipated beauty and barrier, and vulnerability to the unknown" (2015, 272); the organization of the script under three headings – "Play," "Room," and "Relationship" – suggests a communicative capacity for entities not usually attributed either an identity or a voice.

The Play
Name me.
Name me.
Name me.
Describe me.
Diagnose me.
Define me.

The Play
Describe one or more of the following: a breast, a horse, a room, a woman, a land. (2015, 272)

In both of these examples – taken from the play and presented from the point of view of the play – the imperative is used to highlight the text as a site of engagement with what exceeds it. A repetition of the directive "name me" suggests that naming is an iterative and ongoing process, inextricably tied to the processes of reading and / or of interpretation. Rather, that is, than presenting the naming *of* something, Rawlings presents the active process of *seeking* a name. Rather than offering a description, she reveals the imperative for description, diagnosis, and definition at the root of every named thing.

Because no "response" to, or performance of, the play's commands are enacted by the play, the directives remain open, in much the same way that the imperative "know thyself" – which, following Carl Linnaeus's 1735 publication of *Systema Naturae,* remains the only taxonomic "description" of human being – can be interpreted as an open and ongoing address to anyone (or any thing, to follow Rawlings) that has the capacity to listen and self-reflexively engage. This is precisely Rawlings's point. If we refuse to respond for, or to define, what exceeds us – the non-human, the infinite, the unknown – we open ourselves up to the possibility of a generative, indefinite discourse – as well as new ways both of relating beyond, and of recognizing ourselves.

This is because there has existed – long before Linnaeus's time – a vital and fundamental connection between indefinite language and what it quite literally means to be human. In *No One's Ways: An Essay on Infinite Naming*, David Heller-Roazen points to the passage in Homer's *Odyssey* where Odysseus outwits the Cyclops by declaring himself "Outis," or "no one," and states: "In its extreme uncertainty, the name Outis illustrates a fundamental rule of language. Every time the particle 'not' or 'non-' is attached to a given word, the same event in speech may be discerned. One term is denied; its denotations are suppressed. Yet in that refusal, a realm of sense is also disclosed: one that has no positive designation, although it is delimited. Something is named, yet the nature of the naming remains opaque" (2017, 10). For discourses that rely primarily upon descriptive or declarative statements that can be determined as either true or false, the indeterminacy introduced by "non words," or indefinite naming, is often experienced as an impasse or impossibility. For discourses like poetry and prayer, however – those few discourses that, in their reliance on metaphor and imperatives, resist the determination of either true or false – "non-words" become an opportunity for imaginative interpretation. Within a poetic text, for example, the word "not-man," which has flummoxed philosophers at least since Aristotle's discussion of the term in his *Metaphysics*, and has largely been understood to indicate either limit, or lack, may suggest the very real presence of a woman, a child, a glacier, a ghost – or all of the above.

Through its resistance to "positive designation," poetic texts retain the possibility of expressing multiple possibilities and relations, including a relation to the "non-intelligible" – a complex "non-word" defined by the seventeenth century Catalan philosopher Miguel Viñas as that which "negates not only all existing things, but also all possible things, and even more strikingly, all impossible things, however one conceives or reaches them or it" (Heller-Raozen 2017, 101). This term may mark a "land's end in philosophy" that "may never have been surpassed" (2017, 101), but Heller-Roazen's own description of the "non-intelligible" as that which "points, in diverse ways, to … something hybrid and confused, which partakes, impossibly, yet not inconceivably, of quiddity and inexistence" (2017, 100) resounds as a powerful account of poetry's indefinite power.

It is through annulations, evasions, and stammered repetitions that Stevens, for example, evokes a point of indeterminacy between speech and thought that both dismantles and transcends "unitary intellectual meaning." Likewise, Rawlings's emphasis on the inherent contradiction (literally, "against saying / speaking") involved in positive designation – that it denies the subjects and / or objects it "designates" a voice – underscores both the impasse language poses to thought *and* its potential for generating endlessly new relationships to, and configurations of, being.

Concepts like "the pure principle" and "the idea of innocence" that remain undefined in Stevens's "An Ordinary Evening in New Haven" and the open-ended imperatives in Rawlings's *Áfall / Trauma* work to direct the reader past the discursive limits of the text by contradicting or cancelling, rather than positively designating, those limits. In Stevens's "An Ordinary Evening in New Haven," except for the stammering insistence of the speaker ("it is, it is"),[5] the poem seems to indicate that both "the pure principle" and "the idea of innocence" function as "non-words" – pointing not to what exists, but toward the limit point both of experience and its comprehension. Similarly, Rawlings delineates a realm of sense beyond the language she supplies by drawing attention to the physical and temporal limits of our bodies, and to our inadequacies as interpreters of those limits, which we might also understand as imaginative opportunities.

Poetry, as the work of both Stevens and Rawlings attests, is the process wherein thought and speech become disconcertingly blurred; where we are invited to *not-know* where bodies begin and end, or which bodies speak, or how – and to what, or to whom – to listen. It is the overturning of any regime of language and interpretation that would insist on sense over sound, one over many, "as" over "as if." It is the refusal of "positive designation" in the hopes that, via that refusal, "a realm of sense" may be disclosed: "one that has no positive designation, although it is delimited" (Heller-Roazen 2017, 10).

2 "One Kind of Knowledge"

Poetry and Belief

Poetry, writes Muriel Rukeyser, is "one kind of knowledge" that – though it may be "passed between the generations" – is never to be *used* (1996, 7). Rather than a way of looking at lived experience "fact by fact, deriving the connection," it is instead a way of expressing "the relationships themselves" (Rukeyser 1996, 122). It is sustainable precisely because this expression cannot be translated into a series of declarative statements but requires both a point of view and a process of active interpretation. Poetic knowledge may therefore be passed only by making repeated demands on our attention. Although it may refer to or illuminate "the data of human life" (Rukeyser 1996, 122), it ultimately exceeds that data, inviting us to suspend our rational faculties in an act of what Rukeyser terms "faith."

Yes, it takes *faith*, Rukeyser writes, to approach language not as a way of "parceling out" knowledge (1996, 39) but instead as a renewable resource with the capacity to express a larger, if more unstable, truth. It takes faith to rely on our own interpretive capacities – in other words, to believe in ourselves. "Do you accept your own gestures and symbols?"

Rukeyser asks. "Do you believe what you yourself say? When you act, do you believe what you are doing?" (1996, 39). Far from seeking to abstract or to isolate poetic language from "factual" reality through her invocation of "faith," Rukeyser instead expresses her deep commitment to understanding reality as fundamentally poetic.

"Breathe-in experience, breathe-out poetry" (2005, 3), begins "Poem out of Childhood," the first poem from Rukeyser's debut collection, *Theory of Flight* (1935). In this early poem, breath – at once absolutely dependent upon and regulated by the living *corpus*, and also that which always escapes – provides Rukeyser a means of figuring the relationship between both the physical body and the poetic voice, the instantiated present and the unknown future. It also establishes the grounds for her later theories of poetry by demonstrating the corpus as both the site and the agent for potential change.

This is expressed in another early poem from *Theory of Flight*, "In A Dark House," through the figure of "the stairs of a house / builded on stairs" (2005, 9). Rather than converting the verb into its more familiar past tense, "built," Rukeyser's unusual "builded" allows the retention of the active present-tense within an image we simultaneously understand as having been constructed in and by the past. The stairs themselves becomes this complex temporal construction. They exist not only, that is, as the possibility of linear "ascent," but also as a continuing present.

The two figures we encounter on the stairs, "in a house where they had loved / mounting, and the steps a long ascent before them" (2005, 9), are represented in shifting relation to the stairs – which are themselves an expression of constant movement and change. We enter the final stanza, for example, with a "Whir. Whirl of brown stairs" (2005, 9). After having traced the ascent of two people increasingly burdened with private and collective memory, the stanza concludes despondently: "Stupid stupid stupidly stupidly / we go a long voyage on the stairs of a house / builded on stairs" (2005, 9). In the poem's final line, however, this necessary continuance is presented in a more positive light. Here, the poem's central image functions, importantly, both as a concrete description and an abstract imperative: "Steps mount. The brown treads rise. Stairs. Rise up. Stairs" (2005, 9).

What exactly – we may well wonder – can be understood to be "rising" here? Is it the human figures (alternatively evoked within the poem as "he," "she," "we," and "you"), or the stairs themselves? Further: is this "rising" an observable, concrete "fact," or an imperative, the declaration of an ambition or desire? An emphasis on the double function of language – as both representational and an expression of being itself – pervades Rukeyser's poetry. She also underscores the capacity of lyric poetry to establish an "I-thou" relationship between finite subjectivity – the poem's "speaker" – and the infinite, the "other," or non-human objects beyond (Culler 2015, 226). "The voice stems from the body," writes Mladen

Dolar, "but is not its part, and it upholds language without belonging to it" (2006, 73). The "voice" thus "cuts both ways: as an authority over the Other and as an exposure to the Other, an appeal, a plea, an attempt to bend the Other. It cuts directly into the interior, so much so that the very status of the exterior becomes uncertain, and it directly discloses the interior, so much so that the very supposition of an interior depends on the voice" (2006, 80–1). By enacting this "paradoxical topology" (Dolar 2006, 73), Rukeyser's poetry extends "voice" beyond both representation and embodiment – a process that is literalized through the poetic technique of enjambment (a word that comes to us from the French, *enjamber*: "to stride over"). This concrete figuration of the tension and difference between the material limit of language and its signifying possibilities suggests an analogous tension between the "data of human life" and poetic expression.

"Breathe-in experience, breathe-out poetry" (2005, 3), writes Rukeyser. Though contingent upon the "data" or material "fact" of experiential existence, poetry – this line suggests – is always an "excess," a "supplement" to that production. Like the human voice, and being itself, it exists simultaneously outside and inside its defining structure, as both a description of that form and its existential imperative.

"We shall call poetry the discourse in which it is possible to set a metrical limit against a syntactic one," writes Giorgio Agamben. "Prose is the discourse in which this is impossible." Enjambment reveals the "original gait" of poetry, Agamben argues, but also the "gait" of all human discourse;

it thus cannot properly be called either "poetic" or "prosaic." Agamben chooses the word "boustrophedonic," instead, in order to indicate a text that is able to move, at once, both backwards and forwards (1995, 40). The English word for verse – from the Latin word *versura* – points us, similarly, toward a turning point: "the place (and the moment) where the plough turned round at the end of a furrow." Enjambment is thus "an ambiguous gesture that turns in two opposed directions at once: backwards (versus) and forwards (pro-versa). This hanging back, this sublime hesitation between meaning and sound is the poetic inheritance with which thought must come to terms" (1995, 41). Within every "genuine poetic enunciation," Agamben explains elsewhere, there is a simultaneous movement toward sense and sound. It is as if language's movement toward sense is "traversed by another discourse, one moving from comprehension to sound, without either of the two ever reaching its destination" (1999b, 41). Rather than coming to rest in either pure meaning or pure sound, the two meet in a "decisive exchange," each of the two movements following the course of the other: "It is as if, having met each other, each of the two movements then followed the other's tracks, such that language found itself led back in the end to language, and comprehension to comprehension. This inverted chiasm – this and nothing else – is what we call poetry. This chiasm is beyond every vagueness, poetry's crossing with thought, the thinking essence of poetry and the poeticizing essence of thought" (*The End of the Poem* 1999, 41).

In another early poem from *Theory of Flight*, "Effort at Speech between Two People," Rukeyser represents this double movement via a particular emphasis on punctuation. Like several other poems from this collection, the text opens with a colon – suggesting that the content of the poem expands upon or illustrates something that came before. We can understand this anterior statement as either the title of the poem or as a withheld statement, external to the text. In either case, the punctuation mark is inaudible, pointing to the poem's movement away from sound, toward "pure meaning." The colon can be read as the pure promise of that meaning: it indicates that something must and will follow. And yet, on the other hand, the inaudibility of the punctuation mark – the fact that it cannot be voiced, but must be understood instead as a gap, an intake of breath between words – points to the poem's simultaneous movement *away* from sense, toward pure sound.

In *The Life of Poetry* Rukeyser writes: "punctuation is biological. It is the physical indication of the body-rhythms which the reader is to acknowledge" (2005, 117). The colon with which "Effort at Speech between Two People" begins can, accordingly, be understood to indicate that this particular "effort at speech" begins in the body. Before any communication of meaning can be achieved between subjects, there are, first of all, the aspirations of the body: quite literally, *breath*. The colon that marks Rukeyser's own "effort at speech" can thus be understood as a marker of precisely the chiastic crossing described by Agamben between sense and sound – as well as, and more fundamentally, the possibility generated by that crossing. After all, the colon indicates nothing on its own but the existence, beyond what has already been stated, of something yet to come, something *more*.

But the constant tension Agamben refers to – between an idealized notion of a poetry seeking to dissolve meaning in pure sonority and a philosophy seeking to dissolve sonority (and every other material aspect of language) into pure meaning – cannot be understood literally. Instead, the tension is figurative (note Agamben's consistent use of the conditional "it is as if"). Both poetry and philosophy are inextricably bound by, and to, the materials with which they grapple: language, and the perceivable reality it has been developed to represent. Because of this, there is no way of categorically separating the intentions and directions of philosophy or poetry, prosaic meaning or poetic sound. Nevertheless, Agamben's description of poetry as a "chiasma" offers a valuable figure for thinking poetry's unique relationship to both sense and sound – and thus the unique approach poetry affords to representing, and "voicing," the human.

"*Man is the animal*," Agamben writes in *The Open*, "*that must recognize itself as human to be human*" (2004, 26). Although this definition is violently destabilized by the history of colonialism, which systematically polices the borders of the human and restricts the possibility (at least within the bounds of dominant discourse) of self-determination[1] – it also implies an openness to its own revision and redefinition. The human, Agamben suggests, exists always and only "as if" human – is, in other words, capable of assuming the identity only by adopting an interpretive, and self-reflexive, stance. Even then, as poetry inherits and participates in a deeply troubled history of naming and being named, it is also uniquely suited to articulating the possibility inherent to human being: that of refusing systematic definition and of reimagining the ways – and the reasons for which – human being is defined.

In "This Place in the Ways" from *The Green Wave* (1948), Rukeyser dramatizes this tension between the limits of preselected and established forms and their potential redefinition. The speaker of the poem moves rage "for the world as it is" toward love "for what it may be" (2005, 254). In the process, she emphasizes that it is not only her relation to apparent reality but *also* her stance toward what remains unknown that defines her subject position. A space for the subject of the poem is cleared, in other words, through the speaker's own self-reflexive stance toward the possibilities of subjective expression. "And at this place in the ways," the poem concludes:

I wait for song.
My poem-hand still, on the paper,
all night long.
Poems in throat and hand, asleep,
and my storm beating strong! (2005, 254).

Poems exist, Rukeyser assures us here, immanent within subjectivity – even within the structure of the body. The hand is not a hand, but a "poem-hand" – the possibility of its self-expression retained even when silent, at rest.

It is this *possibility* of subjective voicing that Rukeyser seems to celebrate – more even than the instantiation of that possibility in poems or speech. In fact, the speaker even seems to take pleasure in withholding the poem, its retention within – even *as* – the body suggesting the exhilaration of pure and multiple possibility rather than the consummate effect produced through a singular assertion.

Poetry, as Rukeyser demonstrates here and throughout her career, is an investigative effort without any preconceived object. It is a line of questioning without the expectation of an answer, and is itself, continuously and rigorously, placed under question. For Levinas this is the very definition of ethics: "a calling into question" of the limits of the subject through its exposure to "the Other [*l'Autre*]." "The strangeness of the Other," Levinas writes, "his irreducibility to the I [*Moi*], to my thoughts and my possessions, is precisely accomplished [*s'accomplit*] … as ethics" (1969, 43). Elsewhere, Levinas refers to ethics as "a spiritual optics" (1969, 78) – a way of perceiving what exceeds the physical and psychic limits of the eye and the mind.

Understood this way, ethics is also a form of poetry: a way of embodying, of making "present" the fundamental self-reflexivity of human being. It could also be said that poetry is an ethics. That, in enacting the self-reflexive stance integral to human identity and expression and placing the subject under question, poetry provides an orientation and a vocabulary for an ethical way of being in the world.

But what sort of ethics can be applied to a discipline that resists discipline? What truths can be derived from a resistance to or refusal of truth-claims? These questions permeate Rukeyser's best-known work, "The Book of the Dead," from her 1938 collection *U.S. 1*. While still in her early twenties, Rukeyser travelled to Gauley Bridge, West Virginia, in order to report on the now infamous Hawkes Nest Tunnel disaster. Hundreds of workers were dead or dying of silica poisoning as a result of lax, economy-driven safety codes, and Rukeyser was looking for a way of bringing the reality of the situation to light. She had already made something of a name for herself as a journalist, travelling to Spain in 1936 to report on the Spanish Civil War – but it was poetry, rather than journalism, that Rukeyser chose to convey the truth of the Gauley Bridge Disaster. Her journey toward this truth is described in the poem's opening sequence, "The Road," where the figure of a driver consulting a roadmap represents the diverse strategies of depicting reality that lay open to her. In the end, Rukeyser set out – simultaneously – in multiple different directions by employing strategies borrowed from journalism (transcripts, charts, letters, and statistics) alongside more traditional poetic strategies, such as imagery and lyric address. The journalistic elements of the work introduce a factual "juncture" beyond which the lyric elements make a continuous effort to pass. In other words, Rukeyser emphasizes the protean force that gives rise, beyond any citable "facts," to "relationships themselves" (1996, 11) – and a desire for meaning.

The tendency of *poetic* meaning, Rukeyser explains, is toward a holistic response to experience. This holistic, poetic response, is – she adds – also "the most human" response (1996, 41). Accordingly, what Rukeyser asks of poetry, and particularly of its use within the context of social and historical documentation of human events, is that it open up a broad space of self-reflection. Rather than expressing any one truth as such, Rukeyser saw poetry as an opportunity for "imaginative truth" (1996, 135): a way of considering the relationships between multiple perspectives and, as a result of this process, of evoking chance encounters with images or ideas not already known.

"Art," Rukeyser writes in *The Life of Poetry*, "is not in the world to deny any reality. You stand in the cave, the walls are on every side. The walls are real. But in the space between you and the walls, the images of everything you know, full of fire and possibility, life appearing as personal grace … There is here a reciprocal reality. It is the clue to art; and it needs its poetry" (1996, 155). But the "reciprocal reality" onto which poetry sheds light is more difficult to discuss than its counterpart. Unlike the scientist, the craftsman or the technician, the poet has nothing to "show" (1996, 160). The "dramatization" of poetry "in a shock of annunciation" akin to the "dramatization" of science through the discovery of the atomic bomb is impossible because poetry operates through affect rather than effect. As Rukeyser puts it, poetry is "at every instant, concerned with meaning" (1996, 161) – with, that is, the *affective* modes by which we arrive at meaning, rather than the *effective* results of particular meanings.

Poetry, in other words, is interested not in any "Truth" as such, but in its continual "boustrophedonic" approach – not in "Ethics" as a disciplinary category, but in the establishment of an ethical relation. Finally, it is interested not in "History," but in the very material – the observable reality of any given, present moment – from which the future is continuously and actively derived. This, then, is the true function and power of poetry: to give voice to that "most human" belief in continuance, to the power not only of what is, but also of what "is not yet" – in other words, to possibility, and hope.

"Hope," writes the essayist and feminist thinker Rebecca Solnit, "is an embrace of the unknown and the unknowable" (2016, xiv). In direct opposition to what Eve Sedgwick has termed "the paranoid imperative" (2003, 126) – a negative anticipatory mode that assures us there will be "no bad surprises" (Sedgwick 2003, 130) – hope opens onto a space of uncertainty in which there is still "room to act" (Solnit 2016, xi). Hope is the belief, Solnit writes, "that what we do matters even though how and when it may matter, who and what it may impact, are not things we can know beforehand" (2016, xiv).

Both Sedgwick and Solnit share Rukeyser's concern that a pre-emptive or defensive understanding of "reality" as a fixed category located outside of the self, will foreclose on the "fire and possibility" inherent within every instantiation of the real. Sedgwick laments the "anxious paranoid imperative" that dominates contemporary critical thought (2003, 137) and – citing Proust's *Time Regained* as an example – suggests joy as an alternative mode of encountering what exceeds the bounds of human reason. Sedgwick observes that it is only insofar as the multiple and sometimes conflicting truths the speaker of Proust's novel feels "jostling" about inside him cause him joy that he is able to recognize their truth (2003, 137). For twentieth-century literary analysts under the influence of Freud, it would be "inconceivable to imagine joy as a guarantor of truth" (2003, 138), but Sedgwick urges us to revisit the trajectory of paranoid reading Freud's case studies helped institute and direct – and to imagine new, and "reparative," modes of encountering the uncertain and unknown. "To be other than paranoid … does not, in itself, entail a denial of the reality or gravity of enmity or oppression" (2003, 127–8), she assures us. On the contrary: it is an epistemological approach based on the "anticipation of pain" not one based on the "provision of pleasure" that restricts its approach to truth by pre-emptively filling the space that might otherwise have been left available for it. "In a world full of loss, pain, and oppression, both epistemologies are likely to be based on a deep pessimism." Of the two, however, "it is only paranoid knowledge that has so thorough a practice of disavowing its affective motive and force and masquerading as the very stuff of truth" (Sedgwick 2003, 138).

Paranoia, then, in fact retains a deep trust in "the efficacy of truth per se – knowledge in the form of exposure" (2003, 138). It supposes that to acknowledge a problem is the first and necessary step to solving it, thus promoting a linear (if circular) orientation to the very problem it states. It is perhaps for this reason that, as Sedgwick observes, "paranoid knowing is so inescapably narrative" (2003, 138).

The *poetic* imperative can in this sense be understood in direct contradiction to the paranoid imperative Sedgwick describes. Rather than a defensive projection toward a truth revealed through the very act of announcing it (paranoid knowledge as "the very stuff of truth"), Rukeyser demonstrates that poetry is prophetic: "an account of complexities and uncertainties, with openings" (Solnit 2016, xiv).

Like Solnit's hope, Proust's joy, and Sedgwick's "reparative" rather than "paranoid" reading, poetry is "additive and accretive" (Sedgwick 2003, 140) – but rather than a linear expansion toward a projected totality, its accretions extend from, and loop back upon, a subjective point of departure that is necessarily partial, unstable, and temporally limited. It is in this way that poetry can offer an expression of the self-reflexivity fundamental to human being – and produce the grounds for an ethics of hope. It is a resource "never to be used," a way not of producing effects, but of producing *affective* response, a way not of asserting what *is*, but of creating opportunities *within* what is for touching upon the unknown. Like human being itself, it is *boustrophedonic* – a way of moving in opposing directions, and of maintaining, at odds, both sense (the result of meaning) and sound (its sensory, intuitive, and continuous approach).

Here, then, is a reparative practice I'd like to suggest. What if we were to read history, politics, and other of the more "prosaic" methods by which we define ourselves and our relations to the world as essentially *poetic* – and therefore as essentially hopeful? What if we understood that poetry, when it is deeply felt, can speak in the plainest prose – as though it no longer had any need of words?

3 "Un coup de dés"

The Secret History of Poetry – and Its Imaginary Future

In his posthumously published prose work, *Igitur*, Mallarmé opposes the inherent creativity of literary language to the didacticism of rational, and especially mathematical, discourse: "Infinity is born of chance, which you have denied," the speaker of *Igitur* announces. "You, expired mathematicians – I, absolute projection. Should end in Infinity" (Badiou 2005, 20). And yet, as Alain Badiou has observed, mathematics and poetry have a lot in common. Both refuse to acknowledge "the meaning of the claim 'I cannot know'" as well as "spiritualist categories such as those of the unthinkable and the unthought": that which, in other words, we take for granted as exceeding the bounds of human reason (Badiou 2005, 16).

Mallarmé is not wrong, however, to assert that poetic or imaginative infinity provides an escape from mathematical "expiration,"[1] as it is clear that poetry and mathematics hold space for very *different* infinities, and approach them in very different – even opposite – ways. With what follows, I hope to reanimate Mallarmé's faith in the fundamental relation between poetry and the infinite through close readings of the work of the Danish poet Inger Christensen (1935–2009) and the Chamorro poet Craig Santos Perez (b. 1980). I will argue that poetry's self-reflexive concern for the limits of language and subjective experience establishes the possibility of conceiving of, and expressing, the infinite not as a "solution" to finitude, but instead as the absolute contingency that constitutes it.

"A throw of the dice … will never … abolish … chance" (2011, 124, 126, 132, 140), wrote Mallarmé in his famous last poem, "Un coup de dés." Instead, the poem suggests, chance exists outside of the play of circumstance and desire. As Quentin Meillassoux has argued in his book-length "decryption" of this poem, "chance" for Mallarmé cannot be understood in terms of probability or predictability, but instead must be understood as *contingency itself* – that which exists absolutely outside of probability and prescribed knowledge. This is reflected even in the process of "decryption" itself for, though Meillassoux almost exclusively concentrates his attention in *The Number and the Siren* on laboriously demonstrating that the "unique number" referred to in Mallarmé's poem actually *does* exist and that he himself has discovered it (the number, he concludes, is 707), he ultimately asserts that the "uniqueness," and therefore the infinity, of the hidden number lies in the uncertain interpretive act of its having been discovered at all.

Importantly, Meillassoux does not – that is – overlook the fact that his encounter with the "unique" presence of the number 707 within "Un Coup de dés" was made possible only through his own subjective engagement with the text:

it is even possible, he admits, that the number represents his own "unique" interpretation of the poem. But even if it does not – even if Mallarmé carefully calculated and concealed the number 707 within his poem – an element of chance would still, necessarily, be at play in Meillassoux's apprehension of it.[2] What Meillassoux's "decryption" ultimately demonstrates, then, is that rather than begin *or* "end in the Infinite," Mallarmé's poem dissolves a linear and categorical relationship to temporality and subjectivity by rendering legible the inherent contiguities between past, present, and future – as well as between subjectivities (authorial intention and interpretive effect).

The bolded grammatical elements around which "Un coup de dés" is constellated – "AS IF" ("COMME SI"), "IF" ("SI"), and "IT WOULD BE" ("CE SERAIT") – emphasize the contingency upon which every operation (of language, of thought, or of chance) ultimately depends. The poem thus invites the possibility not of definitively naming, but of indicating truth as an ever-present possibility within every act of either representation or interpretation, recalling here that the word indicate "reflects its root image – the index finger – and makes the word into the silently pointing finger … which, saying nothing, hiding nothing, opens up space, opens it up to whoever is open to this arrival" (Blanchot 2007, 40–1).

Inger Christensen's *It* (1969) likewise testifies to the poetic capacity to indicate truth, while ultimately leaving it undefined. Divided into three parts, PROLOGOS, LOGOS, and EPILOGOS, the book exposes the limits of "reason" and "word" and, through that exposition, the immanent potential of human language and thought to move beyond them. There is, of course, an unavoidable association of the word *Logos*, at least in the West, with John 1:1: "In the beginning was the Word, and the word was with God, and the word was God" (Oxford Annotated Bible 1962, 1284). By imagining both a before and an after for "the word," Christensen's text questions and overturns the linear temporality this phrase implies – as well as the presumed suture between word and meaning. Christensen is interested in charting the trajectory of meaning-making as an imaginative and repetitive act rather than a pre-given transcendence and asks us to move both temporally and conceptually beyond both word and meaning in order to arrive at a sense of our role as co-creators of our own histories and possibilities.

PROLOGOS begins with a single sixty-six-line poem, which then steadily breaks down. The second section is made up of two thirty-three-line poems, the third section of three twenty-two-line poems, and so on, until section eight offers a complete reversal of section one, being comprised of sixty-six single-line poems. The effect of this gradual, systematic reduction is that the ordering system of the poem – and the idea of the poem as an ordering system – becomes increasingly apparent to the reader. "It," Christensen begins: "That's it. That started it. It is. Goes on. Moves. Beyond. Becomes. Becomes it and it and it. Goes further than that. Becomes something else. Becomes more. Combines something else with more to keep becoming something else and more. Goes further than that" (2006, 3). The reader is bombarded and overwhelmed by the impossible immensity of what is being named – or rather of what, beyond the ability for "it" to point to anything specific or absolve itself of being merely a word, is being referred to beyond, or prior to, the possibility of naming.

In her introduction to Susanna Nied's English translation of the text, Anne Carson compares the cumulative effect of the poem to what it must have been like "to hear Hesiod in the eighth century BC recite his cosmogonic poems" (2006, ix). Like Hesiod, Christensen wants to "give an account of what is – of everything that is and how it is and what we are in the midst of it" (2006, ix). She is nevertheless aware that in order to go about this she must create a discursive structure that can accommodate, beyond "what is," both what was and what is yet to come.

Number and sequence provide a form for the PROLOGOS section because language cannot yet be relied on at this stage to create its own structures and meanings. It is not until LOGOS that number begins to function as a kind of grammar – but an emphasis on measure and mathematics already in PROLOGOS allows the reader to experience, and imagine, the possible connections between a pre- or non-grammatical system of order and systems of language.

Christensen defines LOGOS as "the word as creative principle, the place where things are consciously staged, put into action, into relationship" (2006, xii) and the segment dedicated to this term is by far the longest, making up 195 pages of the 237-page text. The ordering principle of LOGOS is not mathematics but grammar: Christensen chooses eight categories from a grammatical text called *A Theory of Prepositions* in order to explore the relationship between flux and order within systems of meaning. "I chose eight terms," Christensen writes, "that could stay in a state of flux and at the same time give order to the indistinctness that a state of flux necessarily produces: symmetry, transitivity, continuity, connectivity, variability, extension, integration and universality" (2006, xii).

Each of the poems in LOGOS is associated with one of these eight categories (the words appearing, in sequence, on the top right-hand of the page), as well as with either the term STAGE, ACTION, or TEXT (the words appearing, again in sequence, on the top left-hand of the page.) Even more, perhaps, than in PROLOGOS, the breadth and variety of what it is possible to experience or say about "It" is felt in the multiple shifts of mood, grammar, form, and subject matter contained within these poems. We move, for example, from the taut rhythms of a poem labelled "STAGE / integrities":

> I borrowed a tear from the water
> And wept it again and again
> A fool I had known from the country
> That doesn't exist was my friend (2006, 80)

to an impressionistic inventory (labelled STAGE / universalities):

A happy machine
A wild imagination
A fantastic din
A wheel standing still
You don't notice it
You run for your life
A word that strikes home
The dogs bark (2006, 92)

to the axiomatic (ACTION / transitivities):

Life is holy (2006, 108)

to the colloquial and telegraphic (ACTION / extensions):

Hey clown/stop/it's all within reach/stop/the
stage/stop/ready/stop/has never been so big/stop/hey
stop (2006, 140)

the surrealist confessional (TEXT/continuities):

Today I've been in bed all day. You know they invented
beds. And today they tied us all down (2006, 180)

the associative imagist (TEXT/integrities):

as light that can never
see itself

as none can lie still
falling free

I see your eyes
See (2006, 206)

until, at last, we reach this philosophical conclusion (TEXT/universalities):

I see the weightless clouds
I see the weightless sun
I see how easily they trace
An endless course
As if they trust in me
Here on earth
As if they know that I
Am their words. (2006, 220)

Christensen tests language, mocks it, questions it, celebrates it, succumbs to it … then, finally, as the poem above shows, the speaker accepts her identity as LOGOS. She conceives of her relation to a broader order, or "endless course," by imagining "the weightless clouds … the weightless sun" confirming her existence as a grammatical extension of themselves.

LOGOS is this: the desire for relation and extension. In taking place, it requires a necessary acknowledgement of its own transitiveness, its partiality. "It," in other words, does not exist in LOGOS – or not, at least, as it did in PROLOGOS, as a presumably self-sufficient concept or thing. "It" in LOGOS is always anticipatory. We use it to introduce the possibility of a subject or object and it therefore always exists in relation to subject or object. Christensen's *It* is an exploration of this fundamental relation. Despite the scriptural ambition of the text – to give an account of "everything that is" (Carson 2006, ix) – the poem also demonstrates the limits of accountability. From its initial pronouncement, "It" slides further and further from a direct referent – it multiplies, refracts, is fragmented and dispersed.

And yet "it" does not, Christensen's project suggests, exist without antecedent – or conclusion. Our profoundest realities, just as equally as our barest particles of speech, involve an implicit trajectory – an (even if un-representable, inconceivable) origin and an (even if unimaginable) end. Poetry, for Christensen – and, in particular, this poetic text – is a way of mapping the structure both of poetic language and also of being. *It* explores the relation between the cosmogonic and the cosmologic, between the coming into being of what is (something out of nothing) and the *making sense* of what is.[3] For Christensen, in other words, what can be observed or stated is already a system of meaning, a way of making sense of the world. As Carson writes, "a cosmogony must also be a cosmology," or, more simply, "we are caught in the words we use" (2006, x). But this formula can also be reversed. For Christensen, a cosmology must also be a cosmogony. She shows us that to *make sense* is to employ "the word as creative principle" (2006, xii). It is to generate relations – to consciously make something out of what might otherwise be taken for nothing – and therefore also to orient oneself toward some end. To bring something about (to make something out of nothing) is to already have conceived of the idea of a unit, a whole, and also, therefore, of what exceeds that whole.

Christensen's brief EPILOGOS gives voice to that excess: to what cannot be (or has not yet been) voiced. "That's it," the EPILOGOS begins, "It's the whole thing / It's the whole thing in a mass / It's the whole thing in a mass of difference. It's the whole thing in a mass of different people" (2006, 223). Language and meaning are still cumulative here, but – far from a sense of having arrived at a place of ease or understanding – EPILOGOS is infused with fear and "the whole thing" turns out not to be "whole" at all. "It's the whole thing in a mass of different people / In fear," the text continues. "But it's not a whole. It's nowhere near finished / It's not over / And it hasn't started" (2006, 223). The important thing is not, EPILOGOS urges, "what we are/but what we could / well be / can be / cannot yet be / but can and will be some day" (2006, 227). It is perhaps because of this – because EPILOGOS is poised beyond words, beyond the senses of both reason and the body – that it is a place of absolute vulnerability. The human being must learn "not to subdue the fear," the text urges, because in "eccentric attempts / to move your core / out of yourself / into something else / into others" is the possibility of "making conscious the leap from fear to ecstasy" (2006, 225). Christensen locates this possibility even "in horror / cruelty / murder /orgy/ offering / need / sorrow / fury / poverty / blindness / stupidity" (2006, 225) – in short, in every instance in which the limitations of subjectivity and the body are delineated. "Fear of death / starts everywhere/everywhere in a human being" (2006, 223), writes Christensen. To be human, EPILOGOS suggests, is to be exposed to – to exist as – the possibility of one's own destruction. It is the violent interruption of a subjective temporality – of abstract, "inward-turned visions" that might otherwise disappear in a series of ultimately unfigurable "vanishing points" – with the communal reality of space.

a human being whose face
becomes a much smaller face
vanishing point
for its own vanishing point
in a human being
whose inward-turned visions
return from space
as realities

And the result
the smashed face
a whole of blood and pulverized bone
of fluid from the eyes … (2006, 223)

The human visage is here presented as a physical expression of the violence of self-identification. To recognize oneself as a human subject, the poem implies, is to already have recognized the limitations of subjectivity and the body – and ultimately, its own end. It is to run up against the limit of what the individual human being is not – to smash the finite limits of a body against the infinity of the "pure imagination" (Bachelard 1988, 5).

EPILOGOS is an effort at illustrating and acknowledging the ways in which the violence not only of beginning, but also of ending, is inscribed in every moment of language and being. This final section is permeated with fear because it takes place on the edge – in a space where one body, moment, or layer of meaning endeavours to lose itself in another in order to become something new. Here, bodies become language, and therefore the possibility of different bodies:

when the body
in its blind
sexual
activity
strives to be invisible
the cells are words
when the body
is lost
in it all
and lost
as it is
persists
survives
surpasses

itself
and its limits
the cells are words
when the body
is a thing
the cells are words
when the body
is convulsion. (2006, 234)

"Fear of sex" (2006, 223, 225, 230) gives way to ecstasy, but rather than an atemporal zone "with no point of departure, no end, and no promise," we are viscerally reminded of both the spatial and the temporal structure of language and human being. It is precisely at the height of ecstasy – when "the body / is outside / itself / and / inside / another / illuminated / freed / at peace" (2006, 235) – that we are reminded of the body's cellular structure. Those "cells are words," Christensen writes, "a language / that tells/that the body / can waken / the dead" (2006, 235). "It" is finally realized in EPILOGOS as the space of poetry itself – a discursive form that is as intrinsically connected to the past ("the dead") as it is to the possibility of the future:

how
to let
the cells
in it
proliferate

find their way
to the parallel mouth
lips that speak
as they never
have spoken
as they always
have spoken. (2006, 236)

Whether or not Christensen's poem succeeds in giving account of "everything that is" (2006, ix), it illustrates the protean, poetic possibility of experience and its account: a possibility that is dependent both on the material "reality," including the external limits of the body, and on "inward-turned visions" that depart from those limits; both on the known past (what we "always have spoken") and on the unknown future (what we "never have spoken" – or at least not yet).

"It," Christensen's text assures us, "happens." Like poetry happens. It takes place. But also it is not only what happens, what "falls out." In taking place, poetry presents us with its limits, its (both spatial and temporal) finitude – and thus with the possibility of confronting what exceeds that finitude. It presents us with its own unrealizability – not as an empty gesture, capable of indicating only the futility or failure of language to be true to its word, but as an offering. Poetry is a hand extended – expecting not to be taken, but to be *taken up*, to be translated from the event of its offering into the possibility of kinship.

Craig Santos Perez thematizes this gesture within his remarkable *From* UNINCORPORATED TERRITORY series: *hacha* (Tinfish 2008), *guma'* (Omnidawn 2010), *saina* (Omnidawn 2014), and *lukao* (Omnidawn 2017). Blending documentary and original poetic material and moving fluidly between English, Chamorro, Spanish, and Japanese, as well as between mythic, literary, and historical references, Perez's linked collections provide a (sometimes literal) map of the *poiesis* of history, politics, and cultural identity.

In his preface to hacha, Perez stresses the influence of both definition and resistance to definition, incorporation (embodiment), and what refuses – or is refused – a body, a name, a political identity, or a voice. He begins: "On some maps, Guam doesn't exist; I point to an empty space in the Pacific and say, 'I'm from there'" (2008, 7). He goes on to describe the physical location of Guam ("located at 13 degrees north latitude in the western Pacific Ocean") and then to provide a series of definitions for the term "unincorporated, organized territory" used to describe his native island:

> "unincorporated" because it is an area under U.S. jurisdiction in which only certain "natural" protections of the U.S. Constitution apply; "organized" because the 1950 Guam Organic Act conferred U.S. citizenship and established local government [...] *territory: 1432, "land under the jurisdiction of a town, state, etc" – probably from Latin Territorium: "land around a town, domain, district" – from terra: (see terrain) + -orium, suffix denoting place. Alter-*

nately, the original Latin word suggests derivation from terrere: "to frighten" (see terrible); thus territorium would mean "a place from which people are warned off." (2008, 8)

Incorporated into Perez's poetic work are a range of documentary materials, including excerpts from dictionaries, colonial maps, historical accounts, and contemporary reports on the environment. As John Carlos Rowe has observed: "For Perez, we decolonize effectively when we remember the persistence of colonial forces in our politics and culture" (2017, 218). In order to emphasize the ways in which a construction of identity is often built upon exclusion or refusal, Perez adopts the Spanish word "Reducción" for the (inevitably demeaning) process of arriving at terms of legal, political, and social exchange.

"'Reducción,' Perez informs us, is the term the Spanish used to name their efforts of subduing, converting, and gathering natives through the establishment of missions and the stationing of soldiers to protect these missions" (2008, 11). Likewise – Perez notes – Guam has a history of being "captured (and thus defined) for its strategic position in the Pacific" (2008, 11). He expresses the hope that his poems might "provide a strategic position for 'Guam' to emerge from imperial 'reducción(s)' into further uprisings of meaning" (2008, 11), indicating the importance – both for his politics and for his poetic practice – of both formal structure and its resistance. He concludes his preface to *hacha* by drawing our attention to the multiple valences of the language he employs. An explanation of the non-English Chamorro words is expected perhaps – but Perez finds it equally important to discuss the use of the common English word *from*, in order to think more deeply about notions of origin, as well as about what it might mean to be translated: "*From* indicates a particular time or place as a starting point; *from* refers to a specific location as the first of two limits; *from* imagines a source, a cause, an agent, or an instrument; *from* marks separation, removal, or exclusion; *from* differentiates borders. *From:* OR *'fram,' originally 'forward movement, advancement' – evolving into the sense of 'movement away'*" (2008, 12). The driving concern within Perez's series is the elucidation of these multiple, and evolving, trajectories of language and being. The poems he's chosen to include have "been incorporated from their origins (those 'far flung territories') to establish an 'excerpted space' via the transient, processional, and migratory allowances of the page" (12). This "excerpted space" is made available through Perez's interest in exploring language as a gesture across rather than as an expression or artefact of space and time.

Gaston Bachelard writes that, within poetic form, "actual conditions are no longer determinant … The imagination takes its place on the margin, exactly where the function of unreality comes to charm or disturb – always to awaken – the sleeping being lost in its automatisms" (1964, xxxv). Like Mallarmé and Christensen, Perez questions the distinction between the real and the unreal, and defies the "allowances" of both finite interpretation and the page. His poems range widely, encouraging chance associations between words and meaning. English and non-English text is scattered or "mapped" – like the routes of Spanish galleons (also included) – their arrangement implying multiple possible directions and chains of meaning; blank space is made visible – recovered from the "margins" – by being blocked off and featured prominently at the centre of the text. "Each poem carries the 'from' and bears its weight and resultant incompleteness" (2008, 12), Perez writes, and yet far from a lack, this incompleteness indicates the poems' strength and opportunity. "In the ocean of English words, the Chamorro words in this collection remain insular, struggling to emerge within their own 'excerpted space'" (2008, 12). And yet, it is the "insularity" of the Chamorro words Perez employs – the fact of their being "islanded" on the page – that demonstrates the poetry's capacity of conveying multiple meanings, identities, histories, and possible futures.

An excerpt from *hacha* reads:

in violent
possession ~ i break of
veins
"the last shall be"
forgotten ~
todu i lugát ~
hasa gi tasi ~
(2008, 35)

If we think of this poem as a map, we can see immediately the different possibilities of moving both *from* and *toward* multiple meanings, thereby undoing or unsettling "automatic" interpretations or associations. For example, by excerpting "the last shall be" and islanding it between "veins" (what is incorporated) and "forgotten" (what is refused), the poem disrupts the linear reversal suggested by the well-known teaching from the Gospel of Matthew – "So, the last shall be first, and the first last" (Matthew 20:16) – thus "awakening" the reader ("the sleeping being lost in its automatisms" [Bachelard 1964, xxxv]) to new possibilities, new orders and trajectories. The Chamorro words at the end of the text – doubly islanded, as no translation is offered in this "ocean of English words" – work on multiple levels to draw the language and space of the page into contact with the unknown.

At a literal level, for the English reader who does not have a Chamorro-English dictionary on hand, the words force a confrontation with the limits of language, culture, and subjective interpretation. The words represent (like the delineated blank space above) an uninterpretable block of text, an empty signifier. If translated, the words provide yet another opportunity for contact with what exceeds the finite "allowances of the page." "Todu i lugát" is "everywhere" (Dungca 1975, 253) and "hasa gi tasi" suggests "away in the sea" (Dungca 1975, 90; 41)

Crucial to Perez's poetics is this play between the finite, fixed, and known and the infinite, chance-driven, and unknown. He is determined to ground us: to teach us to locate Guam on a map, to cite historical trade routes, to incorporate his own history ("In 2005, I sit algae mats and fronds across from my grandfather on a small kitchen table in his apartment in Fairfield, California. He talks story about growing up in Guåhan" [2014, 32]), and his own body: "When I lived in Ka'a'awa last summer with my future wife, who's Hawaiian, she seduced me with breakfasts of Corned Beef Hash, hapa rice, and two eggs (any style). For dessert, I consume her body because it's no longer a secret: canned meat is warrior food" (2014, 48). But he is also eager for us to encounter the interface between ground and not-ground, between the body of the subject and the text and what remains literally unincorporated. In a poem called "*from* preterrain" from *saina,* Perez writes:

a map dividing the land covers
my mouth and ears at night
i don't know if i can say our language
                                        will survive here
yet i've never known another place
where history isn't
redressed let our history be seen thru watermarks heard
thru no one speech
will further excavations reveal

'voice' (2010, 36)

This poem depicts the overlay of geographic, political, and corporeal boundaries. We see the speaker and his language marked, "divided" by history, and yet we also see him as an active creator and interpreter. "Yet I've never known another place" suggests an "insular" background and / or attitude toward place, and the idea that the loss of a language native to such a place would be experienced as a devastating lack. But the line breaks and (lack of) punctuation, which allows "Yet I've never known another place" to run into "where history isn't / redressed," suggest that history is inevitably cyclical, and that languages and cultures are themselves "transient, processional, and migratory," engaged in a constant process of destruction and renewal. Read another way (this time imagining "where history isn't redressed" as the beginning of the phrase or thought), the poem suggests the necessity of reading, and thereby recreating, history (in and for the present) even, or especially, in the places where it's been silenced or obscured.

Again, what is important to Perez is the interface between what is and what is not legible or known. His poetry takes place in these interstices, in an "excerpted space" that is nonetheless intricately tied to the larger body it has been excerpted from. We glimpse through his work what other discourses tend to obscure: the connective tissue that binds the known to the unknown, the incorporated and the unincorporated, the material of history to its "redress" through the active imagination.

What Perez calls his poems' "incompleteness" is also, therefore, their ethical stance: poetry is, to return to Mallarmé, "an absolute projection" across space and time – its potential realization always suspended or postponed. The "incompleteness" of a given poem, and its resultant and necessary difficulty,[4] offer opportunities for contact and engagement beyond the poem's formal properties and subjective frame.

Several key aspects of Perez's work make this particularly clear. The inclusion of documentary materials in the text demonstrates – as Rowe has observed, comparing Perez's approach to Muriel Rukeyser's groundbreaking work of documentary poetics, *The Book of the Dead* – that the "discursive complexity" of the work "is a political consequence of imperialism, rather than a testament to the poet's genius" (2017, 220). That is, Perez directs the reader's attention toward the problems and possibilities of discourse within an expansive socio-political and historical context (rather than toward the particular discourse and subjective context of his poems).

The polylingual and polyvocal aspects of Perez's texts further accentuate – and at times enact – the multivalenced, always contingent processes that give rise to systems of meaning. Rowe uses Perez as a key example in his discussion of an "archipelagic" critical methodology that would offer "an alternative ontology for people who have experienced the multiple occupations of colonial powers" (2017, 216). The "archipelagic" methodology Rowe calls for would be one that – beyond creating "contexts for representing discrete and previously minoritized peoples" – would "find points of contact and interrelation that avoid the imperial frameworks and yet respect the cultural, linguistic, and regional differences of these many different regions" (2017, 216).

That Perez's specifically poetic project is chosen by Rowe as his example of this sort of "archipelagic" approach is no accident. Poetry – as, in their very different ways, Perez, Christensen, and Mallarmé all show – affords the possibility of "contact and interrelation" between disparate subjects, as well as between subjects and non-human entities, including their environments. Rather than endeavouring to suture the divide between always-incomplete efforts of speech and the complexity of lived experience, between its own finite form and the infinite or "absolute" that it forms borders upon, poetic texts work to uncover and elaborate this necessarily imbalanced and infinitely contingent relation. In this sense, poetry can be understood not as a rival or exception to more dominant forms of discourse but as a mode of attending to the limitations – and reimagining the possibilities – of every discourse. Its self-reflexive interest in the limits and possibilities of language (as a medium for what the body of any text can – for any number of social, political, psychological, aesthetic, or material reasons – never fully or properly convey) provides a productive site for critique and reflection, as well as for the presentation of new forms of order.

4 The Vanishing Point of Meaning
"Making Sense" of the Fugal Past

M. NourbeSe Philip's retelling or "un-telling" of the *Gregson v. Gilbert* case of 1783, in her experimental text *Zong!* from 2008, is a compelling example of poetry's capacity to extend perspective through and beyond more dominant modes of discourse. Using the only surviving record of the murder of 150 African slaves who were travelling onboard the slave ship *Zong*, Philip's *Zong!* plunges the reader past the impasses presented by legal language and the available historical record by depicting the "vanishing point" of subjective interpretation and experience and thereby reconfiguring our relationship to both language and record.

Philip appeals to her readers to "make sense" both of the language of the *Zong* case and of a historical event that "eludes understanding, perhaps permanently" (Philip 2008, 198). She fragments, disperses, and rewrites a legal document founded upon the systematic exclusion and silencing of the voices her poetic text endeavours to access and express. Emphasized through this experimental presentation is that, without the active involvement of a reader, Philip's effort to give voice to silence – to tell a story "that cannot be told" (Philip

2008, 198) – would be relegated to two dimensions. By underscoring the reader's perspectival and interpretive role in the making, and the propulsion, of meaning, Philip renders visible what mathematician Brian Rotman calls "the artificial rules of linear perspective" (1987, 19), as they pertain to language and history. She also permits us to plunge past these rules – and the constraints they dictate for form and meaning – by configuring her language in such a way that the subjective act of witnessing is restored to a text, and to a context, that violently excludes its subjects.[1]

What we know is this: in 1781, Captain Luke Collingwood set out from the West Coast of Africa for Jamaica with "a cargo" of 470 slaves. Due to navigational errors, the journey lasted four months rather than a mere six to nine weeks, and over the course of that time much of the *Zong*'s valuable "cargo" was lost due to illness and deprivation. Acting on the belief that "it would prove to be more financially advantageous to the owners of the ship" if the slaves were thrown overboard rather than dying natural deaths, Captain Collingwood threw 150 slaves into the sea (Philip 2008, 189). When the ship returned to England, the ship's owners made an insurance claim, seeking to reclaim the value of their lost "cargo," but the insurers refused to pay and the case concluded with the "grotesquely bizarre" ruling that the insurers were indeed responsible for the estimated value of the murdered slaves (Philip 2008, 189).

What we don't know is this: how to "make sense" of this history, and its legacies. Philip's text invites readers to see "further" than the available written record, and the present moment. She does not materially depict anything more, or beyond, that record, but instead both literally and figuratively clears space within the text for the reader's own interpretive processes and act of witnessing. In doing so, she renders explicit the way that poetic texts can work – much like Henri Bergson's "ideal philosophy," described in *The Creative Mind* – to extend our perception beyond immediately recognizable forms.

For Bergson, the ideal would be a way of thinking and seeing that would enable perception to extend beyond the problems and contradictions that naturally arise when confronting the limits of human thought and being. Instead of perceiving these problems and contradictions as a final impasse to thought, or attempting to "rise above our perception of things," we should – Bergson argues – "plunge" into perception instead, "for the purpose of deepening and widening it." Just imagine the possibilities, he exhorts, were we to insert our "will" into perception: "and that this will, expanding, were to expand our vision of things" (2002, 307).

Such a possibility is not without its precedent. For centuries, Bergson reminds us, there have been those whose role has been "precisely to see and to make us see what we do not naturally perceive. They are the artists" (2002, 307). Though Bergson thus recognizes and acknowledges art as a model for his ideal, all-inclusive philosophy – an approach to experience that would throw "an entirely new light" onto psychological and psycho-physiological questions rather than merely make a "cut, for the purposes of practical existence, out of a wider canvas" (2002, 308) – he stops short of acknowledging art *as* this ideal approach.

But Bergson's argument hinges on the supposition that what "would" be philosophy is already art. His claim is that art limits itself to an exploration of surfaces, but his characterization of art as a discipline that "shows us in nature and in the mind, outside of us and within us, things which did not explicitly strike our sense and consciousness" (2002, 307) also suggests the depth-model he conceptually reserves for philosophy. By presenting art as an example of our inherent capacity for moving beyond (either further outside or further inside) what is immediately apparent to our senses, Bergson implies that – even when specifically trading in seemingly impenetrable, indecipherable surfaces – art practice at the very least retains the disciplinary possibility of revealing what is on the other side.

For Bergson, philosophy would, ideally, provide an enlargement of "our vision of things" to such an extent that "nothing in the data of the sense of consciousness would be sacrificed: no quality, no aspect of the real would be substituted for the rest ostensibly to explain it" (2002, 307). It would be a way of seeing so expansive that nothing could be opposed it: "for it would have left nothing outside of itself that other doctrines could pick up; it would have taken everything ..." The impossibility of this ideal is readily admitted: "How can one ask the eyes of the body, or those of the mind, to see more than they see? Our attention can increase precision, clarify and intensify; it cannot bring forth in the field of perception what was not there in the first place" (2002, 307).

And yet, it is precisely this capacity to "bring forth" that Heidegger, drawing from Plato's *Symposium*, identifies as the defining characteristic of *poiesis*, from which we derive our modern term, "poetry." "Every occasion for whatever passes over and goes forward into presencing from that which is not presencing is *poiēsis*, is bringing forth" (1977, 10). Much as the establishment of a vanishing point in the history of the visual arts enabled us to extend our aesthetic perception past two dimensions, poetic language and imagery provide ways of plunging beyond the framework of abstract subjectivity and the present moment. By translating "the infinite into the finite system of language and representation" (Rotman 1987, 19), they work to lend depth and complexity to fixed and linear understandings of subjectivity and time.

This is not a metaphysical process but a perceptual one. By depicting the "vanishing point" of subjective perception within a larger framework – through the figuration of direct address between a speaking "I" and listening "Other," or through linguistic play that troubles ready meaning – poetry acknowledges the real presence of the reader, as well as their role in witnessing and interpreting the presented material. The limit point of the depicted subject, and of discourse itself, is represented within the text – but not for the purposes of interrupting or blocking meaning. By clearing space for the reader's role as both witness and interpreter, poetic texts instead open themselves up to multiplicity, even totality. They create an imaginative field of possibility in which dialectical opposition is abandoned or absorbed and symbolic language and images – or even fragments of them – "make sense," and are perceived, suddenly, as "whole."

This conceptual totality available to poetry is not invulnerable to co-option by totalitarianism – as the example of Heidegger makes clear. But totality is not totalitarianism, and the fact that art, like thought, has often been flattened into dogmatism and decree betrays a problem not in the ambitious agenda of art – that of finding a way to "see further," see "through" – but instead in conceptual interpretations of art that ignore its function as an interface between the finitude of subjective perspective and what lies beyond. To put it another way: totalitarianisms that arise in art result from a problem (either on the part of the artist, the audience, or both) in reading. They manifest when art is construed not as an equation (into which the constant variable is a subjective "point of view"), but as a fixed form, and the imperative of art – its function as a "command addressed to a [reading and/or interpreting] subject" (Rotman 1987, 8) – is obscured or ignored.

In art historical terms, a "vanishing point" can be traced back to experiments conducted by the Italian architect Filippo Brunelleschi in 1425. With the help of a mirror, a canvas, the façade of Florence's famous Baptistery, and the naked eye, Brunelleschi demonstrated "the illusionistic power of linear perspective" (Rotman 1987, 14) – thus marking "the emergence of a code of visual depiction that has dominated all subsequent Western attempts to represent the look of solid, occupiable space by means of a two-dimensional image" (Rotman 1987, 16). Like the number zero, the vanishing point of an image has "a dual semiotic character" (19). Internally, it exists as "a sign among signs" – depicting "a definite location within the real physical scene." Externally, it exists in "metalinguistic relation to these signs," its meaning retrieved only "from the process of depiction itself, from the way the original subjective act of witnessing is represented via the rules of perspective as an image addressed to a spectator" (19).

The "vanishing point," in other words, is the point at which the idea of the infinite is conveyed through the finite system of language and representation. It allows us to "see" past the two-dimensional limits of an image by representing the specific, spatio-temporally grounded site of perception and thus momentarily offering the viewer the possibility of becoming, "via a thought experiment, the artist" (Rotman 1987, 19).

The ideal philosophy described by Bergson is, in effect, a systematization of the talent he ascribes to the artist – that of seeing beyond what we "naturally perceive" (2002, 307). He envisions a philosophical approach that would allow us to widen and deepen our perceptions, and suggests that by questioning the parameters of the readily apparent it may become possible to see more than we currently see.

This perceptual capaciousness (Bergson's ambitious aim for his ideal philosophy) is demonstrated as a logical possibility through the experiments of Brunelleschi. The artist does not create something "out of nothing" (Bergson 2002, 307), nor does she transmit this capacity to her audience. Instead, she adds depth and dimension to her work by making space for the interpretive capacities of the viewer or listener – a process Philip renders literal by fragmenting the language of the *Gregson v. Gilbert* case and scattering it across the page.

As indicated by the example below, Philip's treatment of the legal document in her own text undoes the possibility of a unified meaning that might be arrived at linearly, or in a single direction.

> suspose the law
>   is
> not
>   does
> not
>   would
> not
>   be
> not
> suppose the law not
>   – a crime. (2008, 20)

Philip describes her treatment of *Gregson v. Gilbert* as essentially violent. "I white out and black out words (is there a difference?)," she writes in her commentary on the text.

> – I mutilate the text as the fabric of African life and the lives of these men, women and children were mutilated.
> – I murder the text, literally cutting it into pieces, castrating verbs, suffocating adjectives, murdering nouns, throwing articles, prepositions, conjunctions overboard, jettisoning adverbs: I separate subject from verb, verb from object – create semantic mayhem, until my hands are bloodied from so much killing and cutting, reach into the stinking, eviscerated innards, and like some seer, sangoma, or prophet who, having sacrificed an animal for a new life, or simply life, reads the untold story that tells itself by not telling. (2008, 194–5)

This violent resistance to a discourse that obscures the story Philip wants to tell, but cannot, reveals the possibility of her own specifically *poetic* discourse. In her commentary, Philip admits that she has a deep distrust of the material she works with – language. It is this same material that "promulgated the non-being of African peoples," she writes. And yet, because language's order "hides disorder," because its rationality is "simultaneously irrational," it is also possible to employ language in such a way that it operates outside of or acts as an "exception" to its own rules. "Religious or spiritual communication with nonhuman forces such as gods or supra-human beings" is one example Philip gives of these "exceptional" discourses; "puns, parables, and, of course, poetry" (2008, 197) are others.

Philip's text performs, in her own words: "a wake of sorts, where the spectres of the undead make themselves present" (2008, 201). Her insistence that "only in not-telling can the story be told" is an insistence that only a poetic (prophetic), rather than a rational, approach to language can recover lost histories and voices. Philip's poetic act of recovery hinges not only upon her artistic representation of, and intervention in, the *Zong* case, but also on the way in which that representation and intervention charges the reader or listener with the task of interpretation. Philip's text emphasizes the irrecoverable loss of the story that cannot be told and, simultaneously, the responsibility of the reader to read through and against the surface value of a given text in order to arrive at new forms and meanings. Readers are invited to become artists – to participate in what Bergson called "willed empathy" or "intuition" (Bergson 2002, 220) – and, as a result of this creative process, provide another dimension to the available historical record.

In keeping with Philip's mandate to work only with the language of the *Gregson v. Gilbert* case, her title for the project is simply the more colloquial name for the case itself – but with a specific and crucial difference. Philip adds an exclamation point so that the book's title – *Zong!* – reads less as a label or description and more as an imperative. Philip offers the text to the reader as a cry, a shout, urging the reader to respond to, take up, and further the interpretive intervention she has made.

"Make It New," Ezra Pound declared, famously. And yet this phrase – which has been sourced to a historical anecdote dating to the Shang dynasty – might equally have been interpreted as "Do It Again" (North 2013, 64). The tension between these two interpretations of the same phrase invites us to consider the crucial tension maintained within art and poetry between recurrence and the "New," as well as between discovery and invention.[2]

Philip writes of her engagement with the legal discourse of the *Zong* case:

> I realize that in my approach to this text I have only revealed what is commonplace, although hidden: that even when we believe we have freedom to use whatever words we wish to use … much of the language we work with is already preselected and limited, by fashion, by cultural norms – by systems that shape us such as gender and race – by what's acceptable. By order, logic, and rationality. This, indeed, is also the story that cannot be told, yet must be told. (2008, 198)

Poetry provides for Philip a way of revealing the "commonplace" but more often "hidden" truth about language itself, and of expressing new possibilities for meaning. Poetry does not assign or invent meaning, her text suggests, it invites it; by carving out a "negative space" within a "preselected and limited" structure (2008, 198), poetry opens a space for the future itself to come into being – via the work of the reader, and in the form of the poem.

Philip uses the figure of the fugue to frame her own understanding of the project. "In the musical sense of the word," Philip tells us, "*Zong!* is a counterpointed, fugal antinarrative in which several strands are simultaneously at work" (2008, 204). But there is another, "darker," sense of the word, which is just as pertinent to the project. Fugue also refers to "a state of amnesia in which the individual … [their] subjectivity having been destroyed, becomes alienated from [them]self" (2008, 204). Philip evokes both senses of the word in her stated ambition for the project. By fragmenting the original legal document and re-writing *Zong!* "over it," Philip hopes her text will be read as a "fugal palimpsest through which *Zong!* is allowed to heal the original text of its fugal amnesia" (2002, 204). What might otherwise be a bi-dimensional super-imposition of one writer's interpretation of a text over another becomes an active process where the reader is invited to take on the role of the artist. That is: by directly engaging the reader in the task of "mak(ing) sense" of the work, Philip manages to dramatize not the formal limits of either her text or the original, but the poetic possibility of "bringing forth" what lies beyond every perceivable form. *Zong!* extends perception beyond both presented texts, as well as beyond subjective identity and the present moment, by offering the reader a matrix of possible voices, and points of view.

From the very beginning of Philip's book, the reader understands that she will have to work to "make sense" of the presented material. In the first poem of the first section, "Os" (Latin for "bone" [2002, 183]), for example, we are presented not with a series of readily interpretable words, but with a scattering of letters. On closer examination, we see that the letters can be rearranged to form familiar words: "Water, good / god / one, day." The poems that make up the rest of this first section are labelled in consecutive order ("*Zong! #1*," "*Zong! #2*," "*Zong! #3*," etc.). Though fragmented, they are organized according to discrete units of meaning and laid out in more or less even columns down the centre of the page:

> the some of negroes
>   over
> board
> the rest in lives
>   drowned
> exist did not
>   in themselves
> preservation
>   obliged (2008, 6)

In the second section, "Dicta" (Latin for "a saying," and used in legal discourse to refer to "comments that are pertinent to a case but do not have direct bearing on the outcome" [Philip 2008, 183]), the consecutive numbers drop away so that all the poems in this section are titled simply "*Zong! #*" – their values unknown. By the third and fourth sections, "Sal" (Latin for "salt") and "Ratio" (Latin for "reason," as well as the short form of *ratio decidendi*, "the central reason for a legal decision" [2008, 183]), words, names, letters, and symbols have been dispersed over the entirety of the page and the process of charting meaning among them becomes a more difficult – but also a more potentially various – task.

> & ruth
> etc but
> seal the
> sale & hear
> my tale
> told
> cold sh h (2008, 102)

Where it is still possible to reconstruct a linear pattern for the scattered and sometimes fragmented words presented in these sections, by the fifth section, "Ferrum" (Latin for "iron" [Philip 183]), as the text continues to dissolve and to include more foreign or nonsense words, this possibility is all but withheld:

> the se a the w
> inds for the ta
> te te ta ta for tum de tum for
> a be
> at *o*. (2008, 136)

In the sixth section of the book, "Ebora" (Yoruba for "underwater spirits" [Philip 2008, 184]), the text literally fades into the background – appearing in a grey, rather than a black font – and is often obscured, or written over, by other text.

But then abruptly, at the end of the sixth section, "order, logic, and rationality" (Philip 2008, 198) return. A "glossary" translates words and phrases from fourteen different languages "overheard on board the *Zong*" (2008, 183). A "manifest" appears, ordering lists of words into discrete categories such as "African Groups and Languages," "Animals," "Body Parts," and "Crew" (2008, 184). Finally, a section titled "Notanda" (Latin for "memorandums, notes or observations" [OED 2018]) clearly explains the history and context of the *Gregson v. Gilbert* case, discloses Philip's artistic process, and articulates her ambitions for *Zong!* Far from providing a "solution" to the text, however, the book's final sections introduce additional dimensions against which the reader's interpretive experience is encouraged to refract and reflect. Philip's aim is neither to dictate knowledge nor to generate abstractions. She works to "identify the remains and localize the dead" (Philip 2008, 202), but she does so by exercising the relational possibilities between a range of perspectives and discourses. She performs a "wake" for those who've been lost or systematically denied being, but the performance hinges upon the presence of an engaged reader willing to see further than, and listen beyond, what is possible to "tell."

Philip enacts Bergson's ideal philosophy, or perhaps more accurately she illustrates through *Zong!* that Bergson's ideal was never really a philosophy at all, but a poetics – an invitation to plunge into, and past, the "body of knowledge" (OED 2018), to address it, reinvent it, and mutilate it if necessary. She creates a space within the body of the text in which the reader is impelled to identify their own interpretive subjectivity *within* knowledge. In recognizing the way that subjectivity is inscribed within and as the "vanishing point" of meaning, the reader is also impelled to recognize "the artificial rules of linear perspective" – and, by seeing "further," or "through" them, to arrive at a new relationship to the presented form.

The impasse to rational thought identified by Bergson remains intractable: "How can one ask the eyes of the body, or those of the mind, to see more than they see?" (Bergson 2002, 307). But as Philip's text demonstrates poetry permits perception to expand and extend beyond the limits of rational discourse. One hundred and fifty murdered slaves "make themselves present" (Philip 2008, 201) in the text not because the names Philip has invented for them – names she has written in small print in the margins of the book's first section – align with anything, or anyone, the reader already knows or understands, but because it is the reader herself who must extend her sensibility toward what's been left out. Without ever "making sense" in a rational way, these names and the history they evoke become sensual, proximate. By recognizing and accepting Philip's invitation to responsibility, and involving ourselves within the active process of reading (or un-reading) an untellable tale, *Zong!* directs us toward a recognition of what has been systematically refused being – literally submerged, historically repressed, or denied. It permits us to see past what we "naturally perceive" – to raise the dead and, in doing so, recognize the fugal (many-voiced) form of the future within the fugal (amnesiac) form of the past.

5 "To Undo the Creature"
The Paradox of Writing

The titular section of *Decreation* by Anne Carson is an exploration of the work of three female mystics: the Greek poet, Sappho, from the seventh century BC; Marguerite Porete, a Christian mystic from the fourteenth century; and Simone Weil, the twentieth century author of the concept of "decreation" – the process by which we might pass beyond the limits of the self, in order to move closer to God.

Though made up of thirteen discrete sections of verse and prose, *Decreation* as a whole functions as an investigation into what it means to be human in a very concrete sense. What, Carson asks, are the limits of the human "creature"? Is it possible to confront, even "undo" those limits?

Almost immediately, the investigation flounders. The state of being sought by Sappho, Porete, and Weil beyond the limits of individual identity is necessarily, after all, also a state of being beyond any place from which to "tell" of it. "To tell is a function of self," writes Carson, but when one wants to tell of what exceeds or undoes the "function of the self," it creates "a big problem for the writer" (2005, 172). More than a contradiction, declares Carson, "it is a paradox" (2005, 172).

To demonstrate, Carson provides an excerpt from Porete's religious treatise, *The Mirror of Simple Souls*, for which she was burned at the stake for heresy in 1310:

> For whoever talks about God ... must not doubt but know without doubt ... that he has never felt the true kernel of divine Love which makes the soul absolutely dazzled without being aware of it. For this is the true purified kernel of divine Love which is without creaturely matter and given by the Creator to a creature *and takes away absolutely the practice of telling*. (2005, 173)

But this paradoxical situation that preoccupies Porete – and creates such a problem for the writer – is, very shortly, revealed as the solution. Referring to Simone Weil's phrase, "Eternal beatitude is a state where to look is to eat" (2005, 175), Carson points out that the written page can "reify" the paradox created by the effort of writing beyond the self, thus allowing the writer to "tell" of what is simultaneously both near and far.

In other words, it is by inscribing two paradoxical points of reference (the self and the beyond-self), that the writer is able to communicate the distance – but also the possibility of proximity – between self and beyond-self. In still other words: "the writer's dream of distance becomes an epithet of God" (Carson 2005, 175). It is not, I would suggest, then, so much that writing creates a paradox, but instead that it reveals the paradox at the heart of human being.[1]

For Carson, writing allows the paradoxical possibility of encountering that which remains "incognito" – that which is, in other words, outside, beyond, or uncreaturely about our being – by recognizing the limit between subject and object, self and other. Rather than providing a way of "telling" *of* the uncreaturely or decreaturely, it marks the juncture between the creaturely and the decreaturely – a juncture where what is "incognito" rises to the surface offering the possibility of contact with the known.

In order to illustrate this inverted entry into knowledge, Carson recounts one of her earliest memories: a dream. She recalls observing her childhood living room and experiencing it, from the "sleep-side," as absolutely incognito (unknown). Although objectively, she recalls, it appeared to her the same in every way, the room was "sunk in its greenness, breathing its own order, answerable to no one, apparently penetrable everywhere and yet so perfectly disguised in all the propaganda of its own waking life as to become in a true sense something incognito at the heart of our sleeping house" (2005, 20). To write is to see things in this way, Carson submits: inside out and wrong-way-round. It is to locate the strange within the ordinary – in the same way that a dream permits us to experience the ordinary as strange. It is to confront and address what is invisible, unknown, or has only the most hidden relation to us.

Kafka provides an illustration of this paradoxical commitment within poetic language to what cannot be known or named in "Before the Law" – an enigmatic parable embedded within the text of *The Trial*. The story begins with a man from the country seeking entry into "the law" through a manned doorway. He waits for many years there and even tempts the doorkeeper with bribes, but even so the door remains firmly closed. At the end of the man's life he finally asks: why has no one but me sought out "the law" in all this time? The doorman tells him that no one else could ever have been admitted because the door was constructed only for him and – he concludes – "I am now going to shut it" (Kafka 1998, 217).

It is as impossible to consciously enter into a relationship with "the law," this parable suggests, as it is to absolve oneself of that relationship. And yet, poetic writing affords us the potential to do both. It acknowledges the borders of language and subjectivity at the same time that it thrusts itself beyond them. It embraces the curious and uncertain relation between inside and outside, self and other – interrupting these otherwise flat and impenetrable binaries with a "dream of distance" that, paradoxically, invites what is outside inside, what is categorically other into secret proximity with the self.

"Both the experience of desire and the experience of reading have something to teach us about edges" (1998, 109), writes Carson. Like the man outside the door, which keeps him (alone) shut out, the poem articulates the threshold between language and the non-linguistic, as well as between self and other – thresholds that cannot ultimately be passed. Reflecting on the image of the jealous lover within Porete's mystic writings, Carson describes the way in which this inherent tension – the feeling that what is most desired is being impossibly withheld – actually creates the conditions for a desired "breakdown" of selfhood, or "decreation." "Jealousy is a dance in which everyone moves. It is a dance with a dialectical nature. For the jealous lover must balance two contradictory realities within her heart: on the one hand, that of herself at the centre of the universe and in command of her own will, offering love to her beloved; on the other, that of herself off the centre of the universe and in despite of her own will, watching her beloved love someone else. Naked collision of these two realities brings the lover to a sort of a breakdown" (Carson 2005, 165).

This sort of "breakdown" is experienced by all three of the mystics Carson cites in "Decreation." In Sappho it occurs as the speaker "dislodges" her self from herself: "I am and dead – or almost / I seem to me" (Carson 2005, 159). In both Porete and Weil it occurs as they seek, first psychically, and then physically, to distance themselves from any knowledge or awareness of themselves and their limitations *as* humans. But prior to the "breakdown" of the subject, we have the "naked collision" itself, and something else, too: the residual reverberation of movement and contact with what is other, absent, ineffable, or withheld.

Porete articulates the uncertainty introduced through this contact by coining her own term: "le Loing-prés," which Carson translates as "the FarNear" (2005, 176). The word is not in any way "justified" by Porete, Carson tells us; Porete simply begins to employ it in chapter 58 of *The Mirror of Sim-*

ple Souls, as though its meaning "were self-evident" (2005, 176). In the moment that the soul encounters God, Porete writes, God ravishes the soul, allowing peace to flow into it "like a glorious food." It is "in his capacity as le Loingprés, the FarNear" that God enacts this ravishing – an experience so powerful it "annihilates" subjectivity.

The seeming contradiction of the term, "the FarNear," introduces yet another contradiction into Porete's account. "Where the Soul remains after the work of the Ravishing FarNear, which we call a spark in the manner of an aperture and fast close, *no one could believe*," writes Porete, "*nor would she have any truth who knew how to tell this*" (2005, 176). As Carson points out, Porete cannot help but incorporate into her own "telling" "a little ripple of disbelief – a sort of distortion in the glass – as if to remind us that this dream of distance is after all just a dream" (2005, 176).

But what Carson calls "disbelief" is not so much a wavering of faith as an acknowledgement of the limit-point of language where "telling" becomes "untelling." Narrative is, at this point, abandoned. Porete surrenders her voice to a higher and more resonant frequency – to the "collision" of her own reality, the "known," with that which will always remain "incognito," outside and beyond her. It is the collision of these "two realities" that results in the "annihilation" of individual identity for Porete. By confronting the impassible border of language and selfhood, Porete paradoxically annihilates selfhood. She no longer exists in contrast to, or in tension with, what remains beyond her personal experience, she *resounds* within it.

The simultaneously passive and active response she describes is not a sounding "of" or "as" or "against" some thing, but a *re*-sounding: an echo of that which, outside or prior to consciousness, is already written and understood – so cannot, therefore, be measured from any fixed point of cognition, or narrated according to space or time.

The drive to destroy or dissolve the single self, evident in the work of all three mystics, cannot then be considered separately from their creative impulse to "tell." But what Carson is ultimately able to show is that – rather than revealing a limit or "lack" within either language or being – Sappho, Porete, and Weil reveal the potential for contact and resonance with what lies beyond both.

Despite, that is, an insistence on *lack* as an organizing principle of both eros and poetry, Carson's writing likewise attests to the way that "edges"[2] reveal neither absence nor an objective limit, but instead provide a potential for recognizing – and reconfiguring – relations. In an essay published in the 1995 collection *Glass, Irony, and God* titled "The Gender of Sound," Carson argues that, at least since Greek and Roman times, it has been the definitive tendency of woman to "to put the inside on the outside" (1995a, 136) – to, in other words, disrupt, reverse, or "leak" through the imposed limits of language and law (1995a, 130). "It is an axiom of ancient Greek and Roman medical theory and anatomical discussion that a woman has two mouths. The orifice through which vocal activity takes place and the orifice through which sexual activity takes place are both denoted by the word *stoma* in Greek (*os* in Latin).

Both mouths provide access to a hollow cavity which is guarded by lips that are best kept closed" (Carson 1995a, 131). Indeed, as Carson attests, "putting a door on the female mouth has been an important project of patriarchal culture from antiquity to the present day" (1995a, 121).

Because of this, it is important to understand every expression of "lack" and "limit" within poetry (including Carson's own) as mediated by the patriarchal project Carson refers to, whose business it was to regulate and repress "nonrational sounds" (1995a, 128) both by imposing regulations about who could participate in social and legal proceedings and through written codes (developed in large part to ensure that all signs – rather than messily "leaking" information from the inside of the body out – would "pass through the control point of logos" [1995a, 128]).

Poetry has never cut its tie with the body and continues to be regulated by intuition, interpretation, and breath rather than by logic or decree. An orientation beyond the acknowledged limits of language and selfhood cannot, therefore, be extricated from the history of how, and for what purpose, the line between outside and inside, self and other, linguistic and non-linguistic, has been drawn. It is not *for nothing*, in other words, that Carson has dedicated her poetics to deliberately overstepping this line – to pushing past the implicit boundaries between subjects, genders, genres, and discourses. She does so in order to arrive at new configurations and possibilities for discourse within discourse, and to move toward "another idea of human order than repression, another notion of human virtue than self-control, another kind of human self than one based on dissociation of inside and outside. [And] indeed, another human essence than self" (1995a, 137).

In a short essay from "The Anthropology of Water" – published the same year as *Glass, Irony, and God* – Carson writes: "Sometimes you come to an edge that just breaks off" (1995b, 191). The context is a failing relationship and what reads like a final exchange between two lovers. "I suppose you do love me, in your way," the narrator says. Her lover (described as a "quiet person" who asks "good questions") responds simply: "And how else should I love you – in your way?" (1995b, 191). Within the space of this short exchange, the narrator's attention is redirected from a totalizing view of self to a realization of the spaces within or between self that create the possibility for difference and exchange. This is consistently the function of questions as well as poetic axioms in Carson's work: they work to "break off" the presumed limit to language and subjectivity, revealing the "leakages" *between* presumed limits. Poetry is a way of asking questions and eliciting responses for Carson. Her work recalls a time "when poetry was a way to write philosophy" (Davenport 1995, x), but rather than prescribing a limit to knowledge or the response to any of the questions posed within the structure of her own poetic approach, she seeks to "break off" or "break down" language and subjectivity in order, paradoxically, to emphasize the possibility of contact and relation.

"Surely," writes Carson, as a way of embarking on her "Anthropology of Water," "Surely the world is full of simple truths that can be obtained by asking clear questions and noting the answers" (1995b, 188). The fragmented structure of the essay would seem to undermine or ironize this statement, but the statement is also perfectly sincere in expressing Carson's trust in poetic writing as a way of revealing – and potentially crossing – the distances between self and other, known and unknown, through the simple practice of call and response.

Again, though, what is essential to this practice, for Carson, is that the response not be constrained by the call, the destination by the point of departure. In Carson's introduction to the study of water in her "Anthropology," she writes: "water is something you cannot hold. Like men. I have tried. Father, brother, lover, true friends, hungry ghosts and God, one by one all took themselves out of my hands" (1995b, 117). We then encounter Carson's father in an advanced state of dementia and learn something of the tense relationship she has had with him. Carson portrays both her father and herself as "locked" – unable to communicate except by imposing the "edges" of their own silences and closed worlds on the other. This is exemplified by an anecdote Carson relates about a poem she'd written and left on the kitchen table (titled "I Am an Unlocated Window of Myself") over which her father had written "GARBAGE DAY FRIDAY" some "forty or fifty times" (1995b, 122). With this example, Carson offers a sharp demonstration of both the limits of "patriarchal culture" (1995a, 121) and language (the poet's "call" here elicits a response that obfuscates rather than furthers its potential for interpretation and exchange). The poem becomes a palimpsest, staging several layers of meaning by revealing both the "edges" and blindnesses of writing and its subjective interpretation, as well as the contiguous, as-yet-uninterpreted, space "in between."

Although the father's "overwriting" of his daughter's poem reads like a violent imposition and censuring, the tension this "overwriting" reveals between the two voices and sensibilities also creates a space of possibility and seems to precipitate the daughter's departure from the father's house. Carson writes: "I prayed and fasted. I read the mystics. I began to think I was someone thirsting for God. And then I met a man who told me about the pilgrimage to Compostela. He was a pious man who knew how to ask questions. "How can you see your life unless you leave it?" he said to me" (1995b, 122). Departure is essential for Carson. Even though she notes at the beginning of this same section "I like the people in Kafka's parables. They do not know how to ask the simplest questions" (1995b, 119), it is in fact a willingness to *ask* questions, and via that process of questioning to depart from the known, that Carson celebrates in her work.

Where, that is, the man in Kafka's parable, "before the law," hovers his whole life outside of a single door, without – until the very end – asking the "simplest question," Carson opens the doors we don't even recognize as doors by asking questions of and making departures from received notions of genre, form, subject, and language. Her practice seeks to redraw the boundaries between these categories, thus redirecting possibilities for meaning. For example, in her introduction to "The Anthropology of Water," Carson provides her own definition of the word "anthropology." "To look for the simplest question," she writes, "the most obvious facts, the doors that no one may close, is what I meant by anthropology" (1995b, 123). Carson deliberately – and paradoxically (*anthropos*, coming from the Greek, literally means "human") – extends her anthropology beyond "the study or description of human beings or human nature" (OED 2018, 1) in order to study the relation between the human and the non-human, or (more aptly, perhaps, because more broadly) between formal limits and what escapes or eludes every form. This decision highlights the risk (or "what anthropologists call 'normal danger'" [1995b, 117])[3] associated with any encounter beyond the limits of the subject, but it also calls attention to the unexpected meanings and relations afforded by taking that risk.

Like water, "human beings and human nature" will always elude us, Carson's anthropology suggests. And though she begins her love story with its narrative end, "Father, brother, lover, true friends, hungry ghosts and God, one by one all took themselves out of my hands" (1995b, 117), she also finds a way of sustaining and reading the relationships she thought she had lost. It may, indeed, be impossible to "hold" water, but what we come to understand through Carson's text is that by struggling to contain, or "hold," onto anything – or anyone – we may miss the "obvious fact" that we are being touched by it on every side.

"Love," Carson writes in an entry dated "3rd of July," "is the mystery inside this walking. It runs ahead of us on the road like a dog, out of the photograph" (1995b, 145). Love, in other words – though it is inhuman, profoundly other, and can never be precisely named or grasped – is nonetheless the activating agent within every desire to discover something, to arrive somewhere. Carson's narrative suggests the structural affinities between poetry and the desire for what can never be grasped, but it also suggests that poetry – like love – reveals that there is never any arrival, never any obvious end.

We discover this when, three weeks later in the Compostela account, the narrator arrives at her final destination and, rather than celebrating the conclusion of her journey, reflects on the way that the moment and her experience of it refuses every representation. "At midnight, fireworks in the plaza. No photographs – you know what fireworks are like. Tawdry, staggering, irresistible, like human love" (1995b, 180). The moment refuses every "telling" of itself, cannot be figured except through a consideration of the impossibility of doing so. The fireworks flash and disappear a little like Porete's "Ravishing FarNear, which we call a spark in the manner of an aperture and fast close" (2005, 176). But instead of confirming the limits of language – or of human love ("*nor would she have any truth who knew how to tell this*" [2005b, 176]) – Carson highlights the possibility of arriving at "simple truths" by "asking clear questions and noting the answers" (1995b, 188). At the end of this short entry, for example, Carson concludes with the following inquiry and reply: "When is a pilgrim like the middle of the night? When he burns" (1995b, 180).

The "simple truth" produced through this question and answer pairing does not align with or reflect any established knowledge or relation. Instead, it is a revelation of the "edges" of language and knowledge through the production of a constellation of competing images that invite multiple possible interpretations. Inquiry and response refuse to function logically here, but instead operate more like a zen koan – or like a joke that isn't funny, a riddle not yet solved – where our anticipation of (and desire for) what is familiar or already known is interrupted with the surprise and befuddlement of the unexpected.

On the one hand, we are presented with fireworks – and the associated images of the "staggering" and "irresistible" flashes of human love – and on the other hand, we have the image of absolute darkness, evoked by a question that plunges us, beyond the beauty and brevity of the flashing lights, into "the middle of the night." The image of a pilgrim at the stake, and the whole brutal history surrounding Christian martyrs, is suggested through the question's response: "when he burns."

It may be that the interpretive gap revealed between question and answer is as important as any interpretation. Within the space of this gap, we are nonetheless invited to arrive at a number of simple (and not so simple) truths: 1) the boundaries of knowledge and selfhood are governed and policed; 2) there is, therefore, a great risk in pursuing knowledge beyond the self, which may be punishable by death; 3) truth, like love, and the human experience of time, occurs only in brief flashes; 4) these flashes will (ultimately) destroy you; 5) no matter which direction you head in it will still end in death.

No doubt there are more. In any case, what is brought into sharp focus through Carson's account of her pilgrimage is the difference, and necessary interrelation, between direction and indirection, between narrative or interrogative linearity and the radial "flash" of the poetic image.

A later journey recounted in "The Anthropology of Water" departs dramatically from the Christian pilgrim's model. The narration of an erratic course back and forth across the North American continent seems to be organized primarily not by any notion of geographical progress or direction (despite the frequent reference to maps) but instead by a string of logic from "Classical Chinese Wisdom." As the following example shows, the undated journal entries that make up this section emphasize paradox and seeming contradiction over any sense of a fixed point of either departure or arrival. "Can you be an optimist about nothing?" Carson writes in an entry labelled "Los Angeles, California": "Try. My power is of the kind that belongs exclusively to those without power. *Not explainable then do not explain it,* says classical Chinese wisdom, *not explaining then resolve it without explanation.* An anthropologist's priority is to expose the outside on the inside. It is a tribe lost by finding it, like desire" (1995b, 240).

At one point during this section of the text, the narrator recalls an overheard comment her father made on the eve of her thirteenth birthday. "She isn't going to be one of them," her father had said firmly in response to the topic, "young girls and the dangerous age" (1995b, 235). "Who will I be instead? is a question I never got around to asking Father," writes Carson. "Well I suppose I could be anyone I like or rather, with eyes closed, nobody at all. *A dream dreamt in a dreaming world is not really a dream*, says classical Chinese wisdom, *but a dream not dreamt is*" (1995b, 236).

What interests Carson here, and throughout, is the way in which paradoxes generate a flexibility of the imagination that extends both thought and experience beyond the parameters of language and the presumed limits of both selfhood and knowledge. She demonstrates the way in which the narrator's creature self is "undone" through the paradoxical effort of its account – the way that inside and outside are reversed, that an undreamt dream helps reveal that the world itself is dreaming. Her "anthropology of water" *is* ultimately a study of human life and nature, but it is a poetic study – one entered through the "sleep-side."

Like the dream experience Carson recounts of a childhood living room, what is familiar and known becomes unfamiliar, autonomous, and absolutely exterior to the self – "breathing its own order, answerable to no one" (2005, 20) – and yet, it is this exteriorization, this recognition of the limits of the self that "*takes away absolutely the practice of telling*" that also allows for the possibility of encounter with – rather than discovery of – difference.

It is fitting, then, that "The Anthropology of Water" ends with "An Essay on Swimming by My Brother." Carson departs from her narrator's perspective and deliberately enters the perspective of another. But rather than employing the first person as she does throughout the rest of the text, the protagonist of this essay is described in the limited third person as "the swimmer."

Carson's own estranged brother died suddenly in 2000, five years after the publication of "The Anthropology of Water," but this final section of the text already reads like an elegy for him. "The swimmer" seems at times to be Carson's brother, and at other times to be Carson herself. His most powerful role is, perhaps, as an articulation of their difference – a shadowy and paradoxical figure produced from the "telling" of what (from a limited subject position) cannot be told. Each of the entries in this section are accompanied not by a specific date but by a day of the week, a time, and either the heading "swimming" or "not swimming." We follow "the swimmer" – a solitary and contemplative figure – as he thinks about symmetries, Rilke, and his own "dull life" (1995b, 251). All the while, he swims or does not swim, but in any case we understand his position always in relation to the water's edge. "The swimmer" himself cannot be known; he can only be experienced as a liminal figure hovering in a liminal space. Nonetheless we encounter in "the swimmer" something very real: the desire – both the author's and our own – for an absent beloved. Again, it is not loss or lack that is ultimately represented by either "the swimmer" or the poem as a whole, but instead a paradoxical "FarNear" space of desire and relation.

Fifteen years later we are presented with a new figure for this relation. *Nox* – published ten years after Carson's brother's unexpected death – is conceived of by the author as an "epitaph" with the artefact of the text, as Meghan O'Rourke has suggested, functioning as the "headstone." Indeed, the work "is as much an artefact as a piece of writing" (O'Rourke 2010, np). A reproduction of Carson's own notebook, the text is folded accordion-style, and contains an assortment of poems, prose, photographs, letters, and a practical lexicography. But this seeming fragmentation, which emphasizes both the material (timebound) nature of the work and its tie to Carson's limited subjectivity, belies one of the true functions of the work, which is to provide a "literal" translation of poem 101, the ancient Roman poet Catullus's elegy for his own lost brother. Recalling the only practical advice Benjamin offers in "The Task of the Translator," Carson strives to achieve "transparency" for her translation of the Catullus poem by providing "a literal rendering" of it both through extensive exploration of the meanings of each of the individual words (lexicographical entries are featured on the facing pages of the text) and by representing her own personal investments and experiences of the work – a dimension of translation most translators seek, instead, to hide. Like Benjamin, Carson is concerned not with "resembling the meaning of the original" but with "lovingly and in detail incorporat(ing) the original's mode of signification, thus making both the original and the translation recognizable as fragments of a greater language, just as fragments are part of a vessel" (Benjamin 1968, 78).

She takes Benjamin's advice – that "words rather than sentences" should be "the primary element of the translator" – literally, in order to achieve "the great motif of integrating many tongues into one true language" (1968, 77). But for Carson, the "task of the translator" clearly extends beyond projects involving the translation of one language to another. The impulse that governs her approach to *Nox* – to be "transparent," to find and assemble "fragments of a greater language" – is also evident in "original" work like *Decreation* and "The Anthropology of Water," which seek to express the paradoxical point of contact between what is and what is not possible to tell.

Carson's desire to expose through the "transparency" of her work "a certain fundamental opacity of human being, which likes to show the truth by allowing it to be seen hiding" (*Nox* 2010, np) is rendered literally in another translation, *Antigonick*, from 2012 – the original publication of which featured images printed on transparent paper and overlaid on the text. The illustrations, by the artist Bianca Stone, deliberately avoid direct representation of the events of the play and, because of this, their overlay suggests (like the indirect question and answer pairing from "The Anthropology of Water") an interpretive gap between experience and its representation and underscores the fundamental problems of translation.

For Carson these "problems" have been consistently generative, facilitating rather than thwarting her efforts to explore the "opacity" of human being. Carson's idiosyncrasies as a translator have been sharply criticized, however, by such critics as George Steiner. "Translation," Steiner wrote in his review of *Antigonick*, the opening lines of which included the introduction of modern figures like Hegel, Beckett, and Woolf, "should embody an act of thanks to the original. It should celebrate its own dependence on its source" (2012, np).

But Carson is less interested in showcasing her "dependence on" sources as she is in producing an autonomous text that can function both as a history of its telling and an elegy for what's been lost in the account. "History and elegy are akin," she writes in *Nox*: "The word 'history' comes from an ancient Greek verb ... meaning 'to ask.' One who asks about things – about their dimensions, weight, location, moods, names, holiness, smell – is an historian. But the asking is not idle. It is when you are asking about something that you realize you yourself have survived it, and so you must carry it, or fashion it into a thing that carries itself" (*Nox* 2010, np).

Antigonick's capacity to "carry itself" has been widely recognized. The text has been celebrated by many critics, including Judith Butler and Yopie Prins, not only as a powerful – and faithful – interpretation of the Sophocles original but also as a way of challenging our concept of translation "and the notions of temporality that accompany it" (2015, 136). According to Ben Hjorth, "Carson's apparently 'unfaithful' translation in fact constitutes and performs a challenge to conservative, chronological, teleological temporal frames that constantly threaten to bury the irruptive potential of this text, and this figure, within the deathly chamber of a distant, fixed, 'original' past" (2014, 136).[4] "In just six lines," Prins says – addressing Carson in an interview conducted in 2015 and specifically citing her inclusion of Beckett and Hegel in the opening lines of the play – "you manage to recapitulate a long history of thinking about *Antigone*, and open up new ways to think through the Greek text of Sophocles" (Prins 2015, np). The lines in question (which follow) enact a temporal paradox that emphasizes lexical and temporal opacities and instabilities (Hjorth 2014, 136) while simultaneously allowing the text to speak clearly, in its own voice:

> Antigone: We begin in the dark and birth is the death
> of us
> Ismene: Who said that
> Antigone: Hegel
> Ismene: Sounds more like Beckett
> Antigone: He was paraphrasing Hegel
> Ismene: I don't think so. (2015, 9)

Reading and writing – like human being – is always an act of translation, Carson (and Sophocles, and Hegel, and

Beckett) seems to suggest here, because there is never a point at which we consciously enter into language and relation. There is no way of accessing an "original" or unmediated way of being, but we can, perhaps – by recognizing ourselves as mediated and rendering literal our fragmented languages, subjectivities, and desires – access a "greater language." We can, perhaps – as Carson demonstrates through her work – question the presumed limits of language and self, and, in so doing, encounter both simple truths and unexpected replies.

"Dear Antigone," Carson writes in a preface to the 2015 edition of *Antigonick*, "your name in Greek means something like 'against birth' or 'instead of being born'" (2015, 3). But what is there "instead of being born," Carson asks? The reply: "It's not that we want to understand everything / Or even to understand anything / We want to understand something else" (2015, 3). As the diverse range of Carson's work demonstrates (she is the author of plays, poems, librettos, prose, translation, and many works that purposely defy categorization), poetry is not an aesthetic or generic choice, but a means of understanding "something else," as well as a way of becoming some*one* else ("or rather, with eyes closed, nobody at all" [*Plainwater* 1995, 236]). It is a decreative drama ("note etymology of 'drama' from Greek DRAN 'to do or act'" [Carson, Suicidegirls.com 2012, np]) that in addressing itself to the limits of telling understood as a "function of the self" (2005, 172) paradoxically produces a "collision" with the unknown. Finally, it is a way of perceiving the constant and continuous relation between selfhood and what selfhood can never completely hold: "Father, brother, lover, true friends, hungry ghosts and God" (1995b, 117).

"I keep returning to Brecht," writes Carson, still addressing Antigone, "Who made you do the whole play with a door strapped to your back / A door can have diverse meanings / I stand outside your door / The odd thing is, you stand outside your door too / The door has no inside, / Or if it had an inside, you are the one person who cannot enter it" (2015, 3).

6 *Praxis* and *Poiesis*

The Subversive Structures of Poetry and Human Being

In an effort to establish the primacy of *praxis* over *poiesis*, Aristotle seems to accomplish the reverse of what he intends. In his commentary on Aristotle's *Poetics*, Robert Bernasconi observes that the very act of naming the relation between these two terms radically transforms them by suggesting *praxis* as an end, or "goal," rather than as a spectrum of fluidity and possibility. In this chapter, I want to reclaim this space of error – "error" understood in its Latin sense: "The action of roaming or wandering; hence a devious or winding course, a roving, winding" [OED 2018, 1]). I will argue that the ambiguous relation between *praxis* and *poiesis* Aristotle describes at the heart of human ethics and action is fundamental to both poetry and to human being – and that what is revealed through its equally ambiguous expression is not only the inherent connection between making and doing, or between autonomous and "committed" art, but also the indefinite but nonetheless indivisible bond between subjective truth and objective knowledge, individual accountability and collective responsibility.

"Intellect itself ... moves nothing," Aristotle writes, "but only the intellect which aims at an end [*hou heneka*] and is practical; for this rules the productive intellect [*poiesis*] as well, since everyone who makes makes for an end, and that which is made is not an end in the unqualified sense (but only an end in a particular relation, and the end of a particular operation) – only that which is done [*to prakton*] is that; for good action [*eupraxia*] is an end, and desire aims at this" (Aristotle 1925, VI, 2, 1139a30 to 1139b2, 139). And yet, as Bernasconi asks, "if *praxis* is construed as the goal of *poiesis*, does it not cease to be *praxis*?" (1993, 8). What is even more troubling about this difficult passage, however, is the interpretation (perhaps by Aristotle, and certainly by others – including Bernasconi – after him) of *eupraxia* as a fixed value.

Eupraxia (daughter of Soter, a personification of safety, and Peitharchia, a personification of obedience) was the ancient Greek personification of "doing well," or "good actions or deeds" (Devettere 2002, 45). The employment of this term cannot, therefore, be taken literally, but must be understood as what it is: a poetic figure. If we choose to read eupraxia in this way – not as a fixed ethical code but as a figure open to continuous reinterpretation – we may recognize that, hidden within this short passage, is the *Poetics* Aristotle *didn't* write. This hidden *Poetics* belies Aristotle's straightforward account of "The Anthropology and History of Poetry," in which he describes poetry as having arisen from the "natural" and "universal" pleasure human beings take in imitations (1996, 6). It highlights instead the essentially poetic nature of every serious inquiry into what it might mean to do "well," as well as what it might mean to be human.

"We take delight in viewing the most accurate possible images of objects," Aristotle explains. For, as we view them we "come to understand and work out what each thing is (e.g., 'This is so and so')" (1996, 7). Officially, then, for Aristotle, poetry is a way of representing and intellectually confirming what "is" – what is already known. Anything in excess of this (for example, "if one happens not to have seen the thing [represented] before" [1996, 7]) provides pleasure in a purely aesthetic sense, and – according to Aristotle's presentation – has neither influence nor bearing on what already "is." In these cases, what is represented "will not give pleasure as an imitation, but because of its execution or colour, or for some other reason" (1996, 7). But betrayed by Aristotle's formulation above is that if "the most relevant aspect of human action is its immanent dimension not its external result" (Crespo 2017, 869) then this extends to (and is expressed by) poetry as well. Ethics cannot – this passage suggests – be described, let alone *pre*scribed. Instead, ethical choices must be arrived at through a poetic engagement that translates what "is" into multiple and various possibilities that extend *beyond* what "is" – in the same way that multiple and various interpretations of "good actions or deeds" continue to extend beyond the metaphoric figure for these actions or deeds (*Eupraxia*), which Aristotle supplies. In other words, if we take this passage at its word, what *Eupraxia* denotes is nothing other, or more, than the essential role of metaphor – and the interpretive project it conveys – within every effort of establishing either value or meaning.

Through metaphor, address, and enjambment, poetry upsets a linear interpretation of the relationship between sign and signifier, subject and object, procedure and end. An almost literal "subversion" (under-turning) or "overturning" of *versus* – the "line, row, line of verse, line of writing" – works to reveal not what already "is (e.g., 'this is so-and-so')," but the possibility of what *also* exists, against or in relation to what is represented on the page. Poetry, we could say, subverts its own "ends" by revealing – against and in relation to the material product of the poem – the active process of its own interpretation.

It is this revelation of the material *excessive* of meaning (an attention not just to the verse or poetic "line" itself but to the way that the bend, or turn of verse renders the line legible against an open field) that makes the interpretive project so essential to poetry – and that affords it a unique vantage point for the exploration and critique of more dominant discourses and ideologies of power. Rather, that is, than attempting to suture the relationship between the "this" of signification and the "that" to which signification points, poetry seeks to further disrupt the relationship between signifier and signified, thereby accentuating the interpretive relation at the root of every system of meaning. Because of this, it is not uncommon for the indicative qualities (in other words, the "sense") of language within poetry to fall away – in order either to develop a heightened aesthetic experience, or a disorienting conceptual one. Though far from imitative in a representational sense, this aesthetic and/or conceptual territory nonetheless has direct bearing on what "is" through its expression of the "off-sense" or "non-sense" fundamental to all language, and thus to all truth procedures (before, that is, language – in closing in on meaning – permits such procedures to, in turn, close in on their respective truths).

In Erín Moure's poem "The Unmemntioable," for example, included within her collection of the same name, what cannot be represented through either image or language is evoked through a presentation of the limits of what can. Moure's aim – to subvert ready meaning in order to point within and beyond it to the possibilities it either refuses or contains – is made explicit by the deliberate misspelling in the title of the poem of a word signifying what cannot be named. As the poem progresses, Moure deliberately estranges the reader from his or her own language and subjectivity by disrupting linear relations between grammatical, linguistic, and ontological categories: "what names did I give / those lonely words / before they repeated me? / aside from an outcry / a task of home / my interior vigilant naturally as a horse / on scented pavement / *schmerz*" (2012, 91).

The reader must ask: who is "naming" whom here? Does the subject employ language or is the subject created through a repetition of the language she employs? The defamiliarizing effect of the short lines; the catalogue of images (a cry that emerges from nowhere, an equally displaced home); the unusual associations (home as a task rather than a place, the smell rather than the appearance or texture of pavement); the use of metaphor (an affinity suggested between the speaker's subjectivity and a horse); and the foreign, untranslated words (*schmerz* is the German word for pain) all serve to destabilize a sense of fixity or transparency between the material of language and the activity of meaning-making both within the poem and within established discourse.

In a reversal of Aristotle's definition of poetry as imitative, designed to help us "understand and work out what each thing is" (1996, 7), Moure's poem subverts the possibility of arriving at a single or fixed interpretation. Perhaps because of this paradoxical effort to *de-mean* language, contemporary poetry is often misunderstood (sometimes even by poets) as oriented only *away* from apparent meaning – away, therefore, from anything practical or efficacious, let alone anything that could be called "Truth." I contend, however, that it is precisely poetry's commitment to *avowing* rather than "disavowing its affective motive and force" (Sedgwick 2003, 138) that permits it to access and express the ambiguity inherent within human action and desire – and, by this means, to continuously err toward truth.

Rather than "masquerading as the very stuff of truth" (Sedgwick 2003, 138), poetry is the operation through which the multiple possibilities and permutations immanent within – and beyond – every expression of truth is (potentially) arrived at through the active ("roving, winding") pursuit of its own interpretation. Where one reader might see "nonsense," then, or – on the other end of the spectrum – rote repetition of another discourse, another reader might see a necessary intervention, or the revelation of an essential truth. As Rowe has observed of Craig Santos Perez's *Unincorporated Territory* trilogy, for example, repetition "is necessary, because the history of imperialism, especially in the transpacific region, has produced such discursive and intellectual confusion as to be nearly unreadable" (2017, 222). Perez's strategy of "reiterating key issues" is effective, asserts Rowe, because it permits those issues "to emerge from the white noise of neoimperialism" and allows Perez to "penetrate the distracting screen discourses that occlude the realities of island lives" (2017, 222).

Although not every reader will attend to it in every case, this is poetry's call: to listen closely and read between the lines of what other discourses obfuscate, overshadow, or obscure. Far from moving away from meaning and truth, "nonsense" and repetition – when implemented poetically – are a call to attention: a mode of exploration and experimentation, a way of continuously bending, shifting, and subverting received language and experience in order that it can be encountered anew.

To use another example from Moure's *The Unmemntioable*, Moure does not simply narrate or describe Emmanuel Levinas's "idea of the infinite," she enacts, and thus invites interaction with, the infinite – exposing it in the gap between what can be thought and expressed and what exceeds every intellectual and linguistic effort.

The philosopher Levinas insists that the idea of the infinite in us
consists in a paradox: thinking more than what has yet been thought.

The infinite is not my-idea-of-the-infinite because it exceeds every object
of thought, including its own idea in me.

Thus thought cannot be constrained in the "je" or "I" alone.

Thus the ex-plosivity across membranes. A touch. E.S. and her prosthetic
gesture: language. For if thought that exceeds what has yet been
thought were not possible, the infinite would not be possible, and self/
itself or subjectivity its intermediary transcendence/ incendiary

wooudl collapse (2012, 39).

Once again, Moure presents us with language's limits – its failure to express or represent embodied or material content due to its commitment to abstract categories that refuse specificity. By expressing an idea of "the philosopher Levinas" in the first person ("the infinite is not my-idea-of-the-infinite") Moure exposes the gap not only between finite selfhood and absolute infinity, but also between modes of abstract transcendental thought that systematically exclude the feminine,[1] and the particular transcendences of her embodied, female self. But this breach, or gap, is not exposed simply for the sake of exposure. Nor is Moure's overt, almost comical, disruption of meaning (exemplified by the line "wooudl collapse") a paranoid anticipation of the poem's incapacity to express the idea it intends. Instead, Moure's experimental technique and playful disruptions of the text's "common sense" are a way of highlighting the active and necessary process of interpretation that exceeds but is nonetheless necessary to the delimitation and expression of the poetic material. The question implicit in this poem – how can we even begin to speak of "the infinite," or even of the "self," when systems of language and signification exclude, resist, or collapse under the weight of real bodies? – is answered by the poem itself, which clearly demonstrates the capacity for language, despite or because of its limitations, to "collapse" into new possibilities of signification. Subjectivity and its limited "transcendence/ incendiary" through which it understands itself to be a subject ("constrained by the 'je' or 'I,'") is not fundamentally a defensive position, Moure's poem suggests, but is instead reflexive and contiguous. Language – understood as a "prosthetic," a tool to cross distances rather than expose or define them – can and will survive its inevitable "collapse" against the real. If approached, that is, not as "ends" in themselves, but as component parts in a larger signifying process, both language and subjectivity become not "things" to understand and explain (e.g., 'This is so and so'), but interpretive tools – modes of touching upon, rather than circumscribing, new possibilities of meaning and relation.

To use another example, in Lisa Robertson's "Draft of a Voice-Over for Split-Screen Video Loop" – a 2009 poem that comprises brief assertions, framed as quotations – we listen in on an imagined dialogue, which repeats, refuses, and rearticulates language and imagery associated with traditional femininity in an apparent effort to dislocate the idea of a focal authority or voice and destabilize familiar tropes and language. The aim of the work is not to restrict, negate, or stultify meaning, but rather to point to the complex network of signifying possibilities inherent within even the most rehearsed and internalized ideological language. In 2012 the piece was indeed used as a voice-over for a six-minute split-screen animated video loop created by the artist Amy Sillman. Blending abstract and representational drawings, Sillman's work – like Robertson's – challenges the limits of mimetic form and presents us with new possibilities of reading and interpretation. Both artists share a commitment to "illustrat(ing) the complexities of expressing (or denying) femininity when language itself is a gendered construct" (Hoberman 2009, np) and Sillman's brightly coloured, constantly shifting, often amorphous figures, seem the perfect accompaniment for a poem that announces "none of the forms feel big enough" (Robertson 2009, 46). But, importantly, when the poem is encountered on the page, it is unaccompanied by Sillman's – or any other – illustration. The first lines of the poem therefore describe a visual representation of a figure left visually unrepresented: "'A young woman looks openly out of the picture.' / '*A young woman looks openly out of the picture*'" (2009, 45).

The italicized repetition of this line invites us to look again, not only at the withheld image of the woman the words describe, but also at the various ways in which she has been framed. The fleeting and transitory nature of the image we are (not) being presented with is emphasized by the title's specification that the dialogue is to accompany a cycle of moving images; its partiality and limited perspective are emphasized by the specification of a "split screen." Finally, because we have access only to the (in-progress) "voice-over" and not the images it describes, the poem calls our attention to the absent figure the voice(s) represent – as well as to the fact of the voice's imposition "over" the unrepresented body: "'*Her experience of scale is always paradoxical.*' / 'When girls were flowers this wasn't true.' / '*Her pronoun is sedition unrecognized as such.*' / 'The women is itself not a content'" (2009, 45).

As the cryptic back and forth exchange progresses, the figure we have initially been presented with, peering innocently out of her frame, becomes (as Sillman's illustrations will later show) increasingly fragmented and un-formed. "Scale" is paradoxical for her presumably because she refuses a fixed position. She is not a "still life" of a flower or a pear, but a moving image – not "a content" but a process – and immanent to her identity as a woman is the subversion or refusal of a super-imposed "voice": "'So what if she is thick and stupid behind her life. It is not private.' / '*It can't be regulated.*' / 'No, it is a survival, a learning-to-live.' / '*Knowledge is truth until it's ordinary*'" (2009, 46).

The line between public and private images and realities is made evident here, but not for the purpose of demarcating binary terms. Instead, the poem underscores the complexity and ambiguity of every space through which a line endeavours to be drawn. The presumed fixity of the line draws our attention not to a series of dichotomies, but to the necessary and inherent interrelation between the public and private, the regulated and the unregulated, knowledge and truth. It is up to the unrepresented woman – and it is up to us, the readers – to navigate this difficult terrain, and to negotiate a place for ourselves within it. "'*She exploited a splitting at the level of process*' / 'Her pronoun is sedition unrecognized as such.' / '*She feels free to set out in any discourse*' / 'She doesn't have much time to understand her mortality.' / '*She hasn't been human.*' / 'She wants to tell about it but not necessarily in language'" (2009, 47). By refusing or being denied a category – even that of "human" – the figure is permitted an extraordinary range of movement and possibility, but this too is bounded, the text suggests, by the limits of both her language and her body. Even so, her movement within this bounded space is as seditious as "her pronoun": "'*She imprecisely uses freedom.*' / 'She says space is doubt.' / '*She recycled the discarded part*'" (2009, 48).

What is outside becomes further outside, what is certain becomes uncertain, what is valueless takes on new forms, and therefore new forms of value. Toward the end of the poem, both the possibility of writing and the possibility of the political are extended as powerful tools that move the unrepresented figure away from received notions of femininity and selfhood: "'*She writes against herself.*' / 'She spirals wildly away.' / '*She writes against those who know how to read.*' / 'She feels free to set out in any discourse'" (2009, 49).

The (literally) subversive stance that is being proposed here: a writing through and against the lines of discourse and text is not a repudiation of meaning but a call for new forms of legibility. Truth, the poems suggests, exists outside of prescribed forms of knowledge. It is an unknown quantity – and can therefore be potentially arrived at by anyone, in any discourse. "'*What the political will be to her cannot yet be quantified.*' / 'Knowledge is ordinary.' / '*When women are exiled it feels normal*'" (2009, 50). The challenge I see proposed here, in the poem's final lines, is that of finding an exile from prescribed forms of knowledge that will not seem "ordinary" – and, equally, of finding a way to move outside and against the status quo that will not be read (by others or by oneself) as an acceptance of women's exile. Like Moure, Robertson is interested in deliberately overturning the limitations of an inherited language and drawing attention, instead, to the potentially infinite – if more often hidden – possibilities of language and meaning making. She is interested in presenting what already "is" (philosophical, political, and everyday discourse) in order to reveal, within and against received language and discourse, possibilities that have not yet been, or are just now in the process of, being imagined. As with Moure, poetry for Robertson presents the opportunity for an "explosivity across membranes" – a way of touching upon what exists both immanent within and outside of current concepts and knowledge, or the constraints of "the 'je' or 'I' alone" (2012, 39). Poetic truth, for both poets, does not "end" in the material production of poems. It is a means of revealing within both the subjective and the objective parameters of material production "the immanent dimension" of human language and action and of projecting beyond their "external result" (Crespo 2017, 869). It is not a refusal or erasure of the point of departure (inherited systems of meaning, real historical and socio-political contexts, real bodies, real lives) but it is – from that point of departure – a mode of approach toward a point where, as Cixous writes, "knowing and not knowing touch" (Cixous 1993, 38).

Poetic truth is – the work of Moure and Robertson affirm – an encounter with distance and estrangement. It is a self-reflexive awareness of the subjective limits of language and identity that delimit every discourse. Far from a *dwelling-within*, or a pre-emptive description of the gaps within subjectivity, language, or knowledge – far from the experience of any one of these categories as, in itself, a *lack* – this awareness functions as a (prosthetic) point of contact with other points of departure, systems of meaning, and ways of being.

A poem is, or can be – therefore – both an active process and a thing produced "for-the-sake-of-something." It can be "relative and for someone" – oriented beyond the bounds of what its own discourse can announce or describe. But it can also be "an end in itself" in Aristotle's sense because its ultimate goal can only be achieved through subjective engagement and interpretation. In this way, a poem can be understood as an enactment of the tension and ambiguity between *praxis* and *poiesis* that Aristotle illustrates in his *Ethics* – but rather than the former inevitably governing the latter (as Aristotle's text, perhaps unwittingly, suggests it might), a poem can be read as the subversion and disruption of any presumed hierarchy between doing and making; speaking and listening; autonomy and commitment.

For the poet and the artist, "the color, the bouquet, the tinkling of the spoon on the saucer, are things, in the highest degree" (Sartre 1988, 26), but these "things" are represented and explored (whether imitated or de-meaned) not for the purpose of working out what each one already is, but instead for the purpose of encountering – and even of bringing about – *other* things. What this means is that – contrary to Sartre's assertion that the artist is "as far as he can be from considering colors and signs as a *language*" (1988, 26) – it is precisely the artist's capacity to activate things *as* language that allows "things" to point to other "things," and that allows what "is" to point to what is *also*, what *might* be, or what is "not yet."

In Adorno's rebuttal to Sartre's petition for "committed art" in "What Is Literature," he writes:

> Even in the most sublimated work of art there is a hidden "it should be otherwise." When a work is merely itself and no other thing, as in a pure pseudoscientific construction, it becomes bad art – literally pre-artistic. The moment of true volition, however, is mediated through nothing other than the form of the work itself, whose crystallization becomes an analogy of that other condition which should be. As eminently constructed and produced objects, works of art, even literary ones, point to a practice from which they abstain: the creation of a just life. The mediation is not a compromise between commitment and autonomy, nor a sort of mixture of advanced formal elements with an intellectual content inspired by genuinely or supposedly progressive politics. The content of works of art is never the amount of intellect pumped into them: if anything it is the opposite. Nevertheless, an emphasis on autonomous works is itself sociopolitical in nature. (2013, 360)

It is the artist's, and the writer's, interest in locating and engaging the world as a system of signs that can be constantly re-interpreted that activates even the seemingly "autonomous" work of art, "committing" it – beyond the formal limits of the art object – to the ethical project ("the creation of a just life") and the "it should be otherwise" of sociopolitical engagement. As opposed to a rational discourse that seeks (more or less advertently) to delimit and describe the territory and possibilities of that engagement, poetry proceeds through a process of movement, and error. It extends itself beyond the "made" – beyond, that is, the limits of a text's material structure and any singular "meaning" – but only by acknowledging those limits and rendering palpable the active and ongoing process by which we (continuously) arrive at meaning. Poetry can therefore be understood as a self-reflexive orientation inward, toward its own historical and material structure – but only so far as it is also understood as a projective, even prophetic, gaze outward, toward an external goal that remains external, unquantified, always unknown.

Douglas Kearney explores the tensions and possibilities inherent within this double orientation in his 2015 collection, *Mess And Mess And*. The project, which Fred Moten has called "an anamessianic mess for the end of time that no one can tell us how to use," trudges through the material "mess" of language, history, and the social imagination as it has been imposed on black bodies – in the process calling for new ways of reading and performing.

The book opens with a piece titled "Mess Studies" that meditates upon and re-imagines the distinctions between different forms of refuse – and the possibilities that reside between those distinctions. "Mess is rubbish's cousin, garbage's flesh and blood: akin to what anthropologist Mary Douglas calls *matter out of place* … Perhaps an easy, if messy, way to understand mess is as the passage from Order to garbage. Mess, thus, is liminal" (2015, 18). Kearney's theoretical exploration is interrupted by two pages of handwritten scrawl, inkblots, and blacked out text. Some of the visible text reads: "MESSSS,"

"We see you: Bubbling black; We see you: Runaway black; We see you: Fugitive black," "It's coming fo' sho,'" and "The shit heard round the world" (2015, 20–1). When Kearney performs his poetry he brings clarity and immediacy to what appears "messy," even illegible, on the page. Through performance, Kearney draws attention to the often messy, "liminal" space – between *praxis* and *poiesis* – within which meaning is made and human action is performed.

Like Moure and Robertson, Kearney is interested in enacting the tension between categories of subject and object, doing and making, as well as between endlessness and finite ends. The varied approaches of these three poets to the poem as performance suggests the many different valences of, and possibilities for, poetic truth in relation to the discourse through which it's conveyed. "A poem only becomes poetry when its structure / is made not of words but forces," writes Cecilia Vicuña. "The force is poetry," Vicuña avows, but she specifically withholds a definition of what this force – what "poetry" – is. "Everyone knows what poetry is, but who can say it?" (2012, 121). What is left purposely unsaid here is that "poetry" is the activity of its own interpretation. It is the force of human action in the process of encountering itself as a possibility within and against its own limiting contexts and forms.

Kearney's physical performances of his poetic work function as a mode of interpretation (they are active doings), but they are also further extensions of the "making" of the piece. This ambiguity accentuates the role of the poet and reader within – and as – the truth of the poem. "Poem," Kearney writes. "From the Greek poēma, early variant of poiēma, 'fiction, poem,' from poiein, 'create.' To make. A poem is a made thing. A poem is a made thing. A thing I work to make" (2015, 29). Kearney further emphasizes the doubleness inscribed within this definition through his installations and performances, both of which often invite active participation from the audience. The poem is both a "made thing" and a thing to be made by work or labour. We watch Kearney in the act both of creating the poem and of being created by the poem. His play with language, its multiple meanings, and its potential applications reveal the complicated and terrible history of human discourse, as well as its ongoing complicity with the realities that are created from that history. "Racism is, among other things, a cruelty. Racism, like other stratifying systems of difference, isn't 'just what people do when confronted with an other' – racism requires work. You have to build something, a machine to maintain the cruel, ridiculous institution of it" (2015, 28). Kearney's interest is in revealing the text as a site of performance. His palpable energy and physical use of space on stage, direct eye contact with the audience, and the range of emotion with which he invests his work, makes the text seem inseparable from its performance and from the intimacy that performance generates between speaker and audience. It is not any written record, prior knowledge, or available form that serves as the boundary to language and understanding, Kearney suggests. By disrupting the passive receipt of these forms, modelling a range of interpretive possibilities through the performance of his text, and challenging his readers and listeners to also take up the task of active interpretation, Kearney invites us to both confront the conceptual limits we may not have known we had and, at the same time, to cast beyond them. "Mess Studies," like much of Kearney's work, emphasizes the necessity of a self-reflexive awareness of the ways in which systems of knowledge and power are experienced by, and expressed through, the body. Language and the body do not pose limits for Kearney, but instead provide modes of exploring – and overstepping – the limits imposed by "certain Orders": "I make my poems to make a way through what I often perceive as a mess. This is not the only reason to make a poem, but it's what I'm usually doing. That 'way though' I hope worries certain Orders I find odious – sometime even versions of my own" (2015, 29). The imperative at work within Kearney's poems runs counter to the ideological "Orders" he endeavours to question and disobey. His specifically *poetic* imperative is to recognize the "mess" or disorder inherent to order as well as to "Orders." His work commands self-reflexive attention: "There is a shitload of codes, a mess of messages, yet the din of it isn't necessarily noise – that is, it is a signal to be understood. A literacy to develop" (ibid.). It also impels us to action: "Visitors were directed to add to it using chalk" (20); "If my writing makes a mess of things, it's not to flee understanding, but to map (mis-)understanding as a verb" (29). These directives move us toward an overturning of received language and ideas and encourage acts of self-reflection and imagination rather than prescriptive ways of reading, or the imposition of new "Orders." They uncover within and as what's been "made" of history and language the very work of making. "That mis-a mess," writes Kearney. "And we're in it. Neck-deep. Where the voice-box is" (2015, 29). By inviting us, in this way, to share the role of the "speaker" within the Order-less "mess" of language and history presented in this poem, Kearney invites us toward new enunciations of speaking and being.

Moten calls the text "anamessianic," suggesting a temporality for Kearney's poetry that functions prior to or outside of a messianic expectation of "being saved" or of arriving at an "end." The word connotes the possibility of repetition, reversal, and counter-direction; it calls attention to the way in which poetry like Kearney's operates by pointing both inward (toward the material limits of language, history, and the body) and outward (toward what refuses, or has been refused by, those categories); to the way that it moves both backward (propelled and transfixed by the "mess" of history) and forward (toward the emergent, the possible, the yet to come). "The tradition of the oppressed teaches us that the 'state of emergency' in which we live is not the exception but the rule," wrote Walter Benjamin: "We must attain to a conception of history that is in keeping with this insight. Then we shall clearly realize that it is our task to bring about a real state of emergency, and this will improve our position in the struggle against Fascism. One reason why Fascism has a chance is that in the name of progress its opponents treat it as a historical norm. The current amazement that the things we are experiencing are 'still' possible in the twentieth century is not philosophical. This amazement is not the beginning of knowledge – unless it is the knowledge that the view of history which gives rise to it is untenable" (1968, 257).

Benjamin uses the word "knowledge" here to suggest not the passive receipt of but a definitive break with "a view of history" that gives rise to its own acceptance. His call for a "real state of emergency" is not a call to arms but a call for new directions to thought and language – for ways of attending to the possibility within the rubble or "mess" of every historical moment to bring about real change. I picture Benjamin's "angel of history" being blown back by the chain of events he perceives as "one single catastrophe which keeps piling wreckage upon wreckage" (1968, 257) at his feet – and then I think of Kearney, and Robertson, and Moure, of Craig Santos Perez, Angela Rawlings, M. NourbeSe Philip, Anne Carson, and so many more contemporary poets committed to a different trajectory, a different vision. Their poetry enacts a "state of emergency" in Benjamin's sense. It is a mode of thought and an approach to language that has the potential to reveal – within every discourse and every moment of history – an opening for what has not yet been brought into either action or words. It is an orientation and a responsibility – simultaneously – toward the material facts of language and history and toward truth understood not as a category of knowledge, but as a commitment toward active interpretation and a "being in the direction of chance" (Cixous 1993, 112).

For reasons that I hope this book has shown, it has been more important for most poets to question and destabilize inherited truths than to look for new ones, more important to emphasize the ultimate subjectivity of any one particular point of view than to look for corresponding, or over-arching, objectivity. In speaking here of poetry and truth in the same breath, my intention is not to realign poetry with an old regime of meaning-making from which poets have worked so hard, and for so long, to break away, but instead to recall that poetry (as the best poets in every generation have always made plain) is an orientation toward – and past – the point where "knowing and not knowing touch" (Cixous 1993, 38). It is not, that is, about evasion – a way "to flee understanding" – but is instead an invitation to confront again the indeterminate relation between making and doing fundamental to every human action, including every attempt at defining what "doing well" as a human might mean.

7 The Future Library and the Xenotext

Poetry and the Futurism of the Present

"A forest in Norway is growing. In 100 years it will become an anthology of books." With these words, British artist Katie Paterson introduces us to her "Future Library," a project that curates and supports the production of textual material in two senses. First, Paterson's project is concerned with tending a Norwegian forest and "ensuring its preservation for the 100-year duration of the artwork"; next, it invites contemporary writers to conceive and produce a work "in the hopes of finding a receptive reader in an unknown future" (2019, np).

For a period of over fourteen years, Canadian poet Christian Bök engaged in a similar, if more radical, effort to thrust contemporary art into the unknown. Using a "chemical alphabet," Bök endeavoured to translate a poem into a sequence of DNA with the aim of implanting it into the genome of a bacterium – an extremophile microbe called *Deinococcus radiodurans*, "capable of surviving, without mutation, in even the most hostile milieus, including the vacuum of outer space" (Bök 2011, np).

Once implanted into a cell, Bök's poem would constitute a set of instructions to be interpreted by the organism, prompting the creation of a benign protein. This protein could then be "read," according to Bök's chemical alphabet. "I am, in effect," Bök explains, "engineering a life-form so that it becomes not only a durable archive for storing a poem, but also an operant machine for writing a poem – one that can persist on the planet until the sun itself explodes" (Bök 2011, np).

"Paper texts point backwards," writes Brian Rotman, "they offer to deliver that which has been deposited, something buried in a vault in the past. Their value stems from the promise of this redemption, the possibility of retrieving at least in principle some original full self-affirming 'meaning.'" By contrast, "the xenotext offers no redemption, no written promise of hidden treasure, no icon of value, no delivery of some precious, proto-signifying, species … For the xenotext there is nothing to retrieve; there is only language in a state of potential and never actualised interpretation. What it signifies is its capacity to further signify. Its value is determined by its ability to bring readings of itself into being" (1987, 102).

Though the conceptual projects of Paterson and Bök illustrate two very different approaches to thinking about human agency in relation to what exceeds the time- and space-bound subject, they both figure this fundamentally poetic potential of language and remind us of our own active role as readers and interpreters of the world around us. Without disregarding the constellation of historical, linguistic, and cultural facts that went into shaping the discourses we encounter or the experience of naming and being named, both

Paterson and Bök remind us of the power and responsibility we have to activate and extend the potential of given forms of language and knowledge. In "The Future Library," Paterson's emphasis is on the role of subjective perception in the measure of cosmic and geologic time. Her work directs our attention to the relative nature of all human experience and knowledge, asking us to attend to the possibilities of relation, interaction, and connection – but always within, or as, the space of human experience and thought.

Bök's emphasis in his "Xenotext Experiment" is much more explicitly on what lies beyond subjective interpretation in spatial, temporal, and semiotic terms. He is less interested in expressing the relation between the human and the non-human as a space of engagement and potential action and more interested in gaining access to a highly speculative viewpoint: that of the non-human or the post-human.

When read together, Paterson and Bök's contrasting approaches to the role of human language and agency in the face of the unknown provide a figure for poetry's double orientation: on the one hand toward "timelessness" and the Other (including the non-human object) and, on the other hand, toward the limited resources of the time-bound subject. They offer material representations of the way in which poetry renders the present moment *present* as a literal, and literary, article of transmission and expression – not in order either to stall time, or block the process of future interpretation, but instead in order to illustrate the possibility of interrupting "sequentiality, causality, linear time, [and] teleological meaning" (Culler 2015, 226).

It is by attending to the material limits of the "unknown future" that Paterson figures an encounter with that unknown. She draws our attention to the structure of the book within the form of a young tree, inviting us to read a Norwegian forest as both an infinite poetic resource and a limited natural or material one. In this way, she engages with a temporality that both exceeds and is immanent within our experience of the present – and she allows us to recognize, in the space of that immanence, our own precarious position and immense responsibility.

By casting beyond the human toward an encounter with the non-human that is already inscribed as – and pre-emptively limited by – a particular human subjectivity and linguistic/material form, Bök's "Xenotext Experiment" is, likewise, very much a poem of our time. Its paranoid articulation of the future and ultimate failure to address itself beyond the limits of the subject is simultaneously an invitation to recognize the fact that we exist now, and an opportunity to reflect upon the contingent relation between being and non-being, self and Other.

Where the futurity of most texts remains dependent upon sequence and causality – the projected retrieval, or reconstitution, of meaning from the archive of their presented form – Paterson and Bök demonstrate that it is possible for texts to suspend this "accountability" or "recount-ability" in favour of a literal *response*-ability. Their very different projects oblige us to interrupt or redirect the message contained in the textual materials they present through our own interpretive response.

This vulnerability to unknown, perhaps impossible, future engagements and interpretations is highlighted by both artists through the conception and/or production of withheld art objects.[1] Paterson has intentionally curated her "Future Library" for potential rather than existing readers. The proposed result of Bök's project is doubly withheld. It doesn't and perhaps will never exist – but, were it to exist, it would exist in relation only to a post-human audience.

Paterson invites the reader or interpreter of her project to "see" the future of both forests and libraries and to reflect upon our active role in creating those futures – as well as in stewarding the present and preserving the past. Her figuration of temporality is relatively straightforward: in lieu of a novel by Margaret Atwood or David Mitchell (the first two authors commissioned to compose books for the Future Library) we are presented with a precisely measured delay between the moment of production and interpretation of the art object. The forest, which even as we speak "is growing in Norway," serves as the physical index of this delay.

By postponing the interpretative process to a post-human era rather than a mere one hundred years, Bök's project reveals the supplemental structure of time more starkly. Where Paterson points with her "Future Library" to the potential connectivity of future generations of humans via creative thought, language, and ecology, Bök's *Xenotext* engages with futurity by underscoring the absolute limit point of human language and existence.[2] Rather than revealing a space of vulnerability, however, and/or potential relation between known and unknown, self and other, Bök's project instead works to project a pre-fabricated response into the unimaginable beyond. Were the experiment to succeed as desired, that is, it would be a bacterium's *reply* to Bök's very specific set of instructions – rather than an open address to the unknown future – that would outlast human life on earth.[3] Although it is Bök, not Paterson, who consciously identifies as a poet, the "Xenotext Experiment" may be the less explicitly "poetic" project of the two as, ultimately, Bök ends up compromising the poetic potential of his work in favour of a teleological scientific approach. Far from revealing a "capacity to further signify," Bök's *Xenotext* serves to monumentalize human language and, indeed, human existence on earth.

Bök further emphasizes the divide in his work and thinking between science and poetics through *The Xenotext: Book 1* (Coach House 2015), the project's much anticipated account. Comprised of a mixture of prose and poetry, some of which serves to illustrate the structure of nucleotides, the book is surprisingly reticent on the subject of the book's larger context. Because Bök chooses, in this way, to isolate his textual interpretation of the "Xenotext Experiment" from "poeisis" (i.e., from the ongoing, complex, multi-vocal, and interdiscursive process that gave rise to the production of "poems"),[4] the project seems to present poetry as just another way of expressing a pre-established idea.

But just as Paterson's, Bök's project – understood as a whole – implies conceptual continuities that can only be activated by an engaged reader. The real work of both projects is not, in the end, to deliver a product or result to a future era, but instead to provoke in contemporary audiences a line of inquiry that may include the following questions: will the material chosen for each initiative's projected texts even be a viable form of dissemination within the time frame established by each project (one hundred years in the case of Paterson's Library; an unspecified but definitively post-human era for Bök's)? If either project should achieve a materially transmittable form, will even the most receptive future reader be able or willing to interpret that form according to its own internal conditions and constraints?

In other words, as contemporary readers reflect on the peculiar temporalities figured by both Patterson and Bök, they are confronted with their own very present and very active role as readers in projects that risk, to greater or lesser extents, never otherwise being interpreted at all. If, to offer the more striking example, something like the "Xenotext Experiment" should succeed in actually transcending its contemporary moment and, indeed, human life on this planet, it would first have to be recognized as potentially interpretable. Bök's xenotext therefore figures the possibility of a double indiscernibility: on the one hand, the possibility of appearing structurally equivalent to a mute organism, and on the other of communicating only that it can no longer communicate – operating within a language system that has been rendered obsolete.

At stake here is an even more encompassing question, then: how might we acknowledge, let alone respond to, an address extended to us in a language or a form that is unrecognizable to us, or from a spacetime that is not also our own? Can we, *should* we, attribute forms of speech and writing to non-human entities? Who, and what, can be given voice?

By representing two contrasting tendencies of human thought, along with their attendant risks, Paterson's and Bök's projects demonstrate two opposing, but perhaps ultimately not wholly incompatible, ways of responding to these questions. Paterson's project shows us how a recognition of our subjective limits as partial and particular expressions of a larger, ultimately imperceptible, and inexpressible whole risks circumscribing thought and its creative expression within an endlessly circuitous loop of self-reflexivity. Bök's project, by contrast, shows us how wilfully overstepping the finite bounds of subjective experience and human knowledge risks dogmatically overlaying the subjective over the objective, the particular and the partial over the general and the whole.

Poetry moves us in both directions – on the one hand self-reflexively inward, like Paterson's project, toward a recognition of our limits as subjects and as subjective interpreters, and on the other hand outward, like Bök's project, toward a wilful confrontation with the unknown. Paterson offers us a tangible illustration of poetry's inward orientation. In doing so, she also illustrates the risk we take in reading the world (in the tradition of Jacques Derrida and other deconstructive thinkers) as a system of human communication and exchange we may quite literally never get to the bottom of.[5] Paterson is persuasive, however, in demonstrating the value of self-reflexivity in art and thought. Not only does she encourage us to consider the ways in which both actual and potential knowledge are inscribed within complex systems that exceed us, she also asks us to recognize our role as actors and interpreters within those complex systems. Nonetheless, Paterson's self-reflexive approach to nature and time risks reducing both "the unknown future" and unknown others to players understood primarily as resources available to the human and the contemporary moment.

Bök's *Xenotext* provides a concrete illustration of poetry's outward orientation past the finite limits of knowledge and the linguistic subject. It also, therefore, illustrates the risks of *forgetting* the always partial and particular aspect of human experience and thought and (in the tradition of Badiou, Meillassoux, and others associated with the loosely termed "speculative realist" tradition) unwittingly imposing on the immeasurable and the unknown one's own partial and particular language and point of view. Although Bök's impulse to think and speak beyond the limitations of the present moment and the finite subject is alluring, through his attempt to write a poem capable of outlasting human life on earth Bök unintentionally "overrepresents" himself as if he were not only "the human itself" (Wynter 2003, 260),[6] but also the non- or the post-human.

Forgoing "emotional anecdotes" in favour of "formalistic innovations" (Voyce 2018, np),[7] Bök hopes to lend credence to his discourse by aligning or "fusing" it with modern science. But not only does this position disavow the role lyric poetry has played within the history of innovative poetry, it also leaves unexamined the fact that Bök's stated ambition for the "Xenotext Experiment" – to create an "anomaly" (something that deviates from the expected) structurally strong enough to withstand the onslaught of time and capable of transmitting messages ("alien words") to readers and listeners at unknown distances – is arguably the ambition of every poet and every poem.

Poetry doesn't solve the problems represented by these two opposing poles of human thought – self-reflexively inward on the one hand, self-repudiatingly outward on the other – and every poetic articulation maps its course between these poles with different degrees of success. Adding to the confusion, there is no way of ultimately measuring that success because the degree to which a poem strikes a balance between inward and outward orientations is subject to individual and cultural interpretation that may change dramatically over time.

But the point is that the very structure of poetry offers us a way of exploring, and balancing, two otherwise seemingly conflicted tendencies within thought and its creative expression. Poetry is self-reflexive – implicitly acknowledging, along with Derrida, that "there is no outside-text" (1974, 158) – but it also affords a way to address, and therefore to conceive of contact and exchange with, what remains unwritten.[8]

Of course, poetry does not and cannot presume to speak for or as the other or object of its address, nor can it predict or embody "the unknown future." What it can do is engender a sense of proximity and relation with what – beyond a specific subject's experience, taste, biases, and expectations – might otherwise be considered illegible, or mute. Likewise, although poetry is always, to a certain extent, going to be "the subject of the poem" (Stevens 1966, 144), self-reflexively committed to its status within and as language and within and as a particular point of view, it is also a movement beyond language and subjectivity.[9] Poetic devices such as apostrophe, prosopopeia, and metaphor invite direct confrontation with the limitations of signification and the borders of the speaking subject – and propose ways of traversing them.

It is not, then, through a "hybrid fusion" (Bök 2008, 230) with science – or with any other discipline, for that matter – but instead through an activation of its own (infinite, to follow Rukeyser, "never to be *used*") resources that poetry offers us a way of self-reflexively acknowledging both the power of human thought to imaginatively extend itself beyond the limits of the human and our own time – and the accompanying risks of that extension. By retaining its own double orientation toward and past the limits of the subject, poetry enacts the imperative that defines our own imaginative, and ever-changing, relation to the concepts of selfhood and knowledge. It offers a way of approaching the increasingly urgent ethical and environmental considerations of our time without unwittingly mapping pre-existing knowledge and particular subject placements over unknown others. It affords imaginative proximity, and potential dialogue, with what is barely conceivable, not yet known.

Notes

INTRODUCTION

1 For example, in Aeschylus's *Prometheus Bound*, Oceanus counsels Prometheus: "know yourself," suggesting that by questioning the order of the universe and his place in it he may invite even greater punishment. "Know yourself and learn new ways / For if you fling such sharp and flinty words about / Zeus – even from his far, high throne – may hear / Then these present miseries, this rout / Will look like childish playing (1998, 40).

2 Foucault remarks: "no philosophy, no political or moral option, no empirical science of any kind, no observation of the human body, no analysis of sensation, imagination, or the passions, had ever encountered, in the seventeenth or eighteenth century, anything like man; for man did not exist (any more than life, or language, or labour); and the human sciences did not appear when, as a result of some pressing rationalism, some unresolved scientific problem, some practical concern, it was decided to include man … they appeared when

man constituted himself in Western culture as both that which must be conceived of and that which is to be known" (1970, 344–5).

3 Of Aeschylus, Woolf writes: "To understand him it is not so necessary to understand Greek as to understand poetry. It is necessary to take the dangerous leap through the air without the support of words which Shakespeare also asks of us. For words, when opposed to such a blast of meaning, must give out, must be blown astray, and only by collecting in companies convey the meaning which each one separately is too weak to express. Connecting them in a rapid flight of the mind we know instantly and instinctively what they mean, but could not decant that meaning afresh into any other words. There is an ambiguity which is the mark of the highest poetry; we cannot know exactly what it means" (32).

4 "Poetry, in its original cultural capacity, is born in and as play – sacred play, no doubt, but always, even in its sanctity, verging on gay abandon, mirth and jollity" (Huizinga 2014, 122).

5 Take, for example, William Blake's famous conversation with a sick rose or Whitman's exuberant addresses to life and the infinite: "O Me! O Life!" Other examples include Joy Harjo's directive to an unknown listener: "Remember the sky that you were born under?" or Derek Walcott's address to absent martyrs in "The Sea Is History": "Where are your monuments, your battles,

martyrs?" And Huizinga: "The lyric must be understood here in a very wide sense, so as to include not only the lyrical genre as such but all the moods expressive of rapture. In the scale of poetic speech lyrical expression is the farthest removed from logic and comes closest to music and the dance" (Huizinga 2014, 142).

6 In this essay from 1919 Eliot argues that the "historical sense" of a poet – which he describes as both a sense "of the timeless as well as of the temporal" – is at the same time what makes a writer "acutely conscious" of his own contemporaneity (1998, 28).

7 The dispute between Coleridge and Wordsworth over how far, and for what purposes, poetry should depart from the everyday continues to have lasting influence – enforcing rather than challenging the binary opposition a typical presentation of the famous disagreement presumes between art and life.

8 Auden's famous pronouncement within the poem "In Memory of W.B. Yeats" – "poetry makes nothing happen" – offered a corrective to the common assumption of the literary left during the 1930s that poetry must necessarily be ideological and political (Huddleston 2015). The phrase, especially taken out of context, can easily be misconstrued, however. Rather than disempowering poetry – isolating it from what "happens" in the social and political sphere – Auden's poem instead directs attention to poetry's active role in shaping the possibilities that become our reality.

9 Barbara Johnson argues that poetry's indefinite nature provides an opportunity for expressing the "undecidability" of both human being and the political. "The undecidable is the political. There is politics because there is undecidability" (1986, 35). Poetry, Johnson suggests, expresses this undecidability by "bursting the limits of its own language, inscribing a logic that it itself reveals to be impossible – but necessary" (37).

10 Western culture has harboured a distrust of the "merely" apparent for so long that – as Rei Terada has observed – "to call something apparent is usually to imply dissatisfaction with it" (2009, 9). This, Terada suggests, is largely because fact – in opposition to the "merely" apparent – has become "so deeply conflated with value" (2009, 10). Poetry is interested in interrogating and undoing this conflation – not in order to discount the "facts" of language, subjectivity, and temporality, but in order to acknowledge the contiguous relation of *every* fact to its phenomenal experience and approach and create new orders of association and ways of thinking. Writes Terada: "There's all the difference in the world between natural, inevitable facts or conditions and contingent, temporary ones, yet it's often obscure which are which, and that ambiguity is available to be exploited" (2009, 14). Poetry uncovers the uncertainty surrounding "what counts as a fact" (2009, 14), impelling us to recognize our interpretive complicity in creating systems of value by emphasizing – rather

than refusing or exploiting – the relation between fact and fiction, the apparent and the real.

11 When Heidegger wrote "In poetry, which is authentic and great, an essential superiority reigns over everything which is purely science" (Badiou 2014, 44), he not only betrays an irresponsible approach to both politics and aesthetics, but also a gross misunderstanding of the protean, fundamentally unrestricted possibilities afforded by his own etymological investigations into the root word *poiesis*.

12 Aristotle's *Poetics* (350 BCE), Sir Philip Sydney's *An Apology for Poetry* or *A Defense of Poesy* (1595), Percy Bysshe Shelley's *A Defence of Poetry* (1821), W.H. Auden's "A Short Defense of Poetry" (1967), Marjorie Perloff's "In Defence of Poetry" (1999), and Matthew Zapruder's *Why Poetry* (2017), to name a few.

13 As Tom Fisher notes, Riding's refusal of poetry "took place within a larger critique of disciplinary knowledge, the professionalization of discourse and the mystified authority of a cultural elite. Poetry and philosophy were both on the wrong side of a quarrel with truth." Because of this, Fisher suggests, Riding's renunciation of poetry ultimately "extends rather than extinguishes the possibilities of poetry and permits an exploration of the incarnate, present, materialized worded-ness of the work without the worrying imperative of the impossible 'soundlessness' of truth" (2010, 15).

14 Marianne Moore's 1935 poem "Poetry" famously begins: "I too, dislike it: there are things that are important beyond / all this fiddle / Reading it, however, with a perfect contempt for it, one discovers in / it, after all, a place for the genuine" (2017, 27).

15 Of interrogative thought, Blanchot writes: "The answer is the question's misfortune, its adversity … The question inaugurates a type of relation characterized by openness and free movement; and what it must be satisfied with closes and arrests it. The question awaits an answer, but the answer does not appease the question … [And] in answering, must again take up within itself the essence of the question, which is not extinguished by what answers it" (1993, 14).

16 The "essence" of play is contained in this phrase, writes Johan Huizinga. "But this 'something,'" he continues, "is not the material result of play … but the ideal fact that the game is a success or has been successfully concluded" (2014, 49). Because poetry plays with and against the borders of the subject, the "now," and its own form, what is "at stake" for every poetic project is that it succeeds in being taken up by "something" or "someone" outside the bounds of selfhood, the present moment, and/or the text.

17 Numerous poets and scholars have cited what they see as a resurgence of interest in the power and influence of poetry on contemporary social movements such as Black Lives Matter. In a 2017 article titled "Poetry in a

Time of Protest," Edwidge Danticat harks back to civil rights-era poet and activist Audre Lorde for renewed inspiration in a difficult time: "Poetry," Lorde wrote, "forms the quality of the light within which we predicate our hopes and dreams toward survival and change, first made into language, then into idea, then into more tangible action" (2017, np).

CHAPTER ONE

1 According to Heidegger's formulation of the "fore-structure" of interpretation, we understand something "as" something only by subjecting it to an interpretive process dictated by concepts and forms already available to us. "Interpretation," explains William Blattner, "is directed toward something that falls within the ambit of our understanding, but which is opaque, resistant, or problematic in some way" (Blattner 2007, 14).

2 In *The Sense of an Ending: Studies in the Theory of Fiction*, Kermode argues that Stevens borrowed his "general doctrine of fictions ... from Vaihinger, from Nietzsche, and perhaps from American pragmatism" (1967, 37).

3 To write, Cixous avers, "we must try to unlie. Something renders going in the direction of truth and dying almost synonymous. It is dangerous to go in the direction of truth. We cannot read about it, we cannot bear it, we cannot say it; all we can think is that only at the very last minute will you know what you are going to

say, though we never know when the last minute will be" (1993, 36).

4 Blanchot explores the generative potential of the "negative space" of reading and writing in Chapter XVIII of *The Infinite Conversation*, "The Absence of the Book": "the first one to write, the one who cut into stone or wood under ancient skies ... What he left behind was not something more, something added to other things, it was not even something less – a subtraction of matter, a hollow in relation to a relief. Then what was it? A gap in the universe: nothing that was visible, nothing invisible. I suppose the first reader was engulfed in this non-absent absence, but without knowing anything about it" (1993, 422).

5 For Deleuze, the effect of the "stutter" within a written text is discussed as a mark of literary acumen and originality and the successful "stutter" is an example of "when *saying is doing*" (1998, 107). "This is what happens," Deleuze explains, "when the stuttering no longer affects pre-existing words, but itself introduces the words it affects; these words no longer exist independently of the stutter, which selects and links them through itself. It is no longer the character who stutters in speech; it is the writer who becomes *a stutterer in language*. He makes the language as such stutter: an affective and intensive language, and no longer an affectation of the one who speaks" (1998, 107). He continues: "Creative stuttering is what makes language

grow from the middle, like grass; it is what makes language a rhizome instead of a tree, what puts language in perpetual disequilibrium: *Ill Seen, Ill Said* (content and expression). Being well spoken has never been the distinctive feature or the concern of great writers" (1998, 111).

CHAPTER TWO

1 Poetry's indefinite self-reflexive stance is inseparable from the ongoing history of slavery and from other human rights abuses that rely upon and systematically promote a sense of relativity at the heart of what it means to be human. As Sylvia Wynter attests, it was the "systemic stigmatization, social inferiorization, and dynamically produced material deprivation" of the "Native" and "Black" Other that served to "'verify' the overrepresentation of Man as if it were the human, and to legitimate the subordination of the world and well-being of the latter to those of the former" (2003, 267).

CHAPTER THREE

1 Mallarmé was wrong "on at least one point," writes Alain Badiou. "Like every great poet, Mallarmé was engaged with a tacit rivalry with mathematics. He was trying to show that a densely imagistic poetic line, when articulated within the bare cadences of thinking,

comprises as much if not more truth than the extra-linguistic inscription of the matheme" (2005, 20).

2 Mallarmé would have had to decide, for example, what "counts." Is it the total number of words in the poem? Or the number of syllables? Might punctuation marks "count," too? And what about compound words? Importantly, the compound word upon which the "fixity" of Meillassoux's count founders (upon which determinacy, trembling with indeterminacy, incorporates that indeterminacy within itself and, at last, becomes – once and once only, in a single, finite act – *chance itself*) is "peut-être."

3 As Carson notes, the terms cosmology and cosmogony "are sometimes used interchangeably in English, but they are not the same. Cosmogony, from *kosmos* ('cosmos') and *gignesthai* ('to come into being'), refers to the birth of things out of nothing. Cosmology, from *kosmos* and *logos*, means the system by which things make sense to us" (2006, x).

4 Referenced here is, of course, T.S. Eliot's famous pronouncement from "The Metaphysical Poets": "We can only say that it appears likely that poets in our civilization, as it exists at present, must be difficult. Our civilization comprehends great variety and complexity, and this variety and complexity, playing upon a refined sensibility, must produce various and complex results. The poet must become more and more comprehensive, more allusive, more indirect, in order to force, to

dislocate if necessary, language into his meaning" (1932, 248).

CHAPTER FOUR

1 "Even if," writes Philip in her commentary on the text, "the courts had found against the owners of the Zong and ruled that they could not claim insurance compensation, given the law at that time, neither Captain Collingwood nor those who had helped in the massacre could be charged with murder, since what was destroyed, being property, was not capable of being murdered" (2008, 191).

2 "The essential fault of surrealism," wrote Wallace Stevens in 1942, "is that it invents without discovering. To make a clam play the accordion is to invent and not to discover. The observation of the unconscious, so far as it can be observed, should reveal things of which we have previously been unconscious, not the familiar things of which we have been conscious plus imagination" (1966, 919).

CHAPTER FIVE

1 In the words of Marguerite Duras, writing is "the pace of the written word passing through your body. Crossing it. That's where one starts to talk about those emotions that are hard to say, that are so foreign, and yet

that suddenly grab hold of you" (2011, 73). For her, in other words – as for Cixous and Carson – writing is not about being descriptive or elucidatory, but instead about posing an active challenge to the perceived limits of language and selfhood. It is for this reason that "there are often narratives but very seldom writing" (2011, 72) and that "the writing of literature is what poses a problem to every book, to every writer, to every writer's every book" (75).

2 "As eros insists upon the edges of human beings and of the spaces between them, the written consonant imposes edge on the sounds of human speech and insists on the reality of that edge, although it has its origin in the reading and writing imagination" (Carson 1998, 55). Inherent – in other words – to the act of recognizing and articulating an "edge" of either selfhood or words is an encounter with what refuses (or is refused) definition.

3 "It was an anthropologist that first taught me about danger," Carson writes. "He emphasized the importance of using encounter rather than (say) discovery when talking about such things" (1995, 117).

4 Carson herself insists on the work as a translation rather than a "rewriting" of the classic work. "I don't see any 'rewrite' going on," she said in an interview. "Everything I've done in the translation is an attempt to convey a move or shock or darkening that happens in the original text. This doesn't always mean repro-

ducing the words and sentences of the original in their same order, but a play is (note etymology of 'drama' from Greek DRAN 'to do or act') a collection of actions or doings, this is what needs to be rendered from Greek into English. It's true Sophokles doesn't mention Hegel on the first page of Antigone, but he does refer to the long tradition of A's catastrophic family in order to remind his Greek audience of the legend and for us, in 2012, the Antigone legend includes Hegel" (Suicide-girls.com 2012, np).

CHAPTER SIX

1 Levinas's subordination of the woman as "Other" is famously critiqued by Simone de Beauvoir in *The Second Sex* as anti-feminist. After quoting the following passage from Levinas's essay "Time and the Other": "[Alterity] is accomplished in the feminine. The term is on the same level as, but in meaning opposed to, consciousness," de Beauvoir writes: "I suppose Mr. Levinas is not forgetting that woman is also consciousness for herself. But it is striking that he deliberately adopts a man's point of view, disregarding the reciprocity of the subject and the object. When he writes that woman is mystery, he assumes that she is mystery for man. So this apparently objective description is in fact an affirmation of male privilege" (de Beauvoir 2011, 8).

CHAPTER SEVEN

1 "The poem does not aim, nor describe, any object, or objectivity," writes Badiou (2014, 28). Instead, it aims toward a "complete de-objectification" (2014, 31) of the text or art object that renders palpable the *actual* presence within every moment of the possible future.

2 Writes Paterson: "The timescale is … not vast in cosmic terms. However, in many ways the human timescale of one hundred years is more confronting. It is beyond many of our current lifespans, but close enough to come face to face with it, to comprehend and relativize" ("The Future Library").

3 So far, the translation process Bök is looking for has "worked properly" (Bök 2015, 150) in *E. Coli* bacteria, but not yet in "the intended symbiote … *D. radiodurans* (a germ able to survive, unchanged, in even the deadliest of environments)" (Bök 2015, 150).

4 "All along," Joshua Schuster writes in his review of the work, "it was understood that the poem was not going to be a verbal icon, and not the book either, but the work of the poem in its trying to get made" (2016, np). And yet, strangely, this broad framework ("Poeisis included: all the computer programming, grant writing, art exhibits, promotional tweets, interviews, preposterous claims, raised eyebrows and bioethical murmurings" (Schuster 2016, np)) is noted only briefly at the

back of the text in a section titled "Vita Explicata" (Bök 2015, 150).

5 "The formal essence of the sign can only be determined in terms of presence. One cannot get around that response, except by challenging the very form of the question and beginning to think that the sign ~~is~~ that ill-named~~thing~~, the only one, that escapes the instituting question of philosophy: 'what is … ?'" (Derrida 1974, 18–19).

6 Well into the modern era, the category "Man" has gone relatively unexamined – continuing, as Sylvia Wynter has written, to "[overrepresent] itself as if it were the human itself" (2003, 260).

7 In an interview, Bök explains: "I began writing poetry in my late adolescence, producing work inspired mostly by the likes of Michael Ondaatje, Leonard Cohen, and Gwendolyn MacEwan. I published some of this juvenilia, but I became convinced late in my undergraduate career that, if I continued writing emotive, lyrical anecdotes, then I was unlikely to make any important, epistemic contributions to the history of poetry" (Voyce 2018, np).

8 As Marian Hobson has noted: "even if 'text' is interpreted widely, to include or even to privilege non-linguistic traces, there nevertheless has to be a looping back into language from the not-quite or already-not-linguistic. Though that utterance was revised in

the second publication of *Limited Inc.* to imply 'there is nothing outside the context,' we are still within the linguistic web" (1998, 201).

9 The line is taken from Stevens's 1937 collection, *The Man with the Blue Guitar:* "Poetry is the subject of the poem / From this the poem issues and / To this returns. Between the two / Between issue and return, there is / An absence of reality, Things as they are. Or so we say" (1966, 144–5). Elsewhere, Stevens reflects in prose: "The themes of life are the themes of poetry. It seems to be, so clearly, that what is the end of life for the politician or the philosopher, say, ought to be the end of life for the poet, and that his important poems ought to be the poems of the achievement of that end. But poetry is neither politics nor philosophy. Poetry is poetry, and one's objective as a poet is to achieve poetry" (1966, 808).

References

Adorno, Theodor. 1983. *Prisms: Essays in Cultural Criticism and Society.* Edited by Shierry Weber Nicholsen and Samuel Weber. Cambridge, MA: MIT Press.

– 2013. "Commitment." *A Practical Reader in Contemporary Literary Theory.* Edited by Peter Brooker and Peter Widdowson. London, UK and New York, NY: Routledge.

Aeschylus. 1998. *Prometheus Bound.* Translated by Paul Roche. Wauconda, IL: Bolchazy-Carducci Publishers.

Agamben, Giorgio. 1995. *Idea of Prose.* Translated by Michael Sullivan and Sam Whitsitt. Albany, NY: State University of New York Press.

– 1999a. *The Man without Content.* Translated by Georgia Albert. Stanford, CA: Stanford University Press.

– 1999b. *The End of the Poem: Studies in Poetics.* Translated by Daniel Heller-Roazen. Stanford, CA: Stanford University Press.

– 2004. *The Open.* Translated by Kevin Attell. Stanford, CA: Stanford University Press.

– 2010. *The Sacrament of Language: An Archaeology of the Oath.* Translated by Adam Kotsko. Palo Alto, CA: Stanford University Press.

Altieri, Charles. 2013. *Wallace Stevens and the Demands of Modernity: Toward a Phenomenology of Value*. Ithaca, NY: Cornell University Press.

Aristotle. 1925. *The Nicomachean Ethics*. Translated by David Ross. Oxford, UK and New York, NY: Oxford University Press.

– 1996. *Poetics*. Translated by Malcolm Heath. New York, NY and London, UK: Penguin Classics.

Austin, J.L. 1962. *How to Do Things with Words*. Edited by J.O. Urmson and Marina Sbisà. Cambridge, MA: Harvard University Press.

Bachelard, Gaston. 1964. *The Poetics of Space*. Translated by Maria Jolas. Boston, MA: Beacon Press.

– 1988. *Air and Dreams: An Essay on the Imagination of Movement*. Translated by Edith R. Farrell and C. Frederick Farrell. Dallas, TX: The Dallas Institute Publications.

Badiou, Alain. 2005. *Theoretical Writings*. Translated by Ray Brassier and Alberto Toscano. New York, NY and London, UK: Continuum.

– 2014. *The Age of the Poets*. Translated by Bruno Bosteels. New York, NY and London, UK: Verso.

Barthes, Roland. 1985. *The Responsibility of Forms: Critical Essays on Music, Art, and Representation*. Translated by Richard Howard. New York, NY: Hill and Wang.

Benjamin, Walter. 1968. *Illuminations: Essays and Reflections*. Translated by Harry Zohn. New York, NY: Schocken Books.

Bergson, Henri. 2002. *Key Writings*. Edited by Keith Andell

Pearson and John Ó Maoilearca. Translated by Melissa McMahon. London, UK: Bloomsbury.

Bernasconi, Robert. 1993. *Heidegger in Question: The Art of Existing*. Atlantic Highlands, NJ: Humanities Press.

Blanchot, Maurice. 1993. *The Infinite Conversation*. Theory and History of Literature, Vol. 82. Translated by Susan Hanson. Minneapolis, MN and London, UK: University of Minnesota Press.

–2007. *A Voice from Elsewhere*. Translated by Charlotte Mandell. Albany, NY: State University of New York Press.

Blattner, William. 2007. "Ontology, the A Priori and the Primacy of Practice: An Aporia in Heidegger's Early Philosophy." In *Transcendental Heidegger*, edited by Stephen Crowell and Jeff Malpas. Stanford, CA: Stanford University Press.

Bök, Christian. 2008. "The Xenotext Experiment." *SCRIPTed* 5, no. 2 (August): 227–31.

–2011. "The Xenotext Works." Poetry Foundation, 2 April 2011. https://www.poetryfoundation.org/harriet/2011/04/the-xenotext-works.

–2015. *The Xenotext: Book 1*. Toronto, ON: Coach House Books.

Carlos Rowe, John. 2017. "'Shades of Paradise': Craig Santos Perez's Transpacific Voyages." Essay in *Archipelagic American Studies*. Edited by Brian Russell Roberts and Michelle Ann Stephens. Durham, NC: Duke University Press.

Carson, Anne. 1995a. *Glass, Irony and God*. New York, NY: New Directions.

– 1995b. *Plainwater*. New York, NY: Vintage.

– 1998. *Eros the Bittersweet*. Champaign, IL and London, UK: Dalkey Archive Press.

– 2005. *Decreation: Poetry, Essays, Opera*. New York, NY: Alfred A. Knopf.

– 2006. Introduction to *It*. Inger Christensen, ix–xv. New York, NY: New Directions.

– 2010. *Nox*. New York, NY: New Directions.

Christensen, Inger. 2006. *It*. Translated by Susanna Nied. New York, NY: New Directions.

Cixous, Hélène. 1993. *Three Steps on the Ladder of Writing*. Translated by Sarah Cornell and Susan Sellers. New York, NY: Columbia University Press.

Crespo, Ricardo F. 2017. *Economics and Other Disciplines: Assessing New Economic Currents*. London, UK and New York, NY: Routledge.

Culler, Jonathan. 2015. *Theory of the Lyric*. Cambridge, MA and London, UK: Harvard University Press.

Danticat, Edwidge. 2017. "Poetry in a Time of Protest." *New Yorker*, 31 January 2017. https://www.newyorker.com/culture/cultural-comment/poetry-in-a-time-of-protest.

Davenport, Guy. 1995. "Introduction." In *Glass, Irony and God* by Anne Carson, vi–x. New York, NY: New Directions.

De Beauvoir, Simone. 2011. *The Second Sex*. Translated by Constance Borde and Sheila Malovany-Chevallier. New York, NY: Vintage Books.

Deleuze, Gilles. 1998. "He Stuttered." In *Essays Critical and Clinical*, translated by Daniel W. Smith and Michael A. Greco. New York, NY and London, UK: Verso.

Derrida, Jacques. 1974. *Of Grammatology*. Translated by Gayatri Chakravorty Spivak. Baltimore, MD and London, UK: The Johns Hopkins University Press.

Devettere, Raymond J. 2002. *Introduction to Virtue Ethics: Insights of the Ancient Greeks*. Washington, DC: Georgetown University Press.

Dolar, Mladen. 2006. *A Voice and Nothing More*. Cambridge, MA and London, UK: MIT Press.

Dungca et al. 1975. *Chamorro-English Dictionary*. Honolulu, HI: University of Hawaii Press.

Duras, Marguerite. 2011. *Writing*. Translated by Mark Polizzotti. Minneapolis, MN and London, UK: University of Minnesota Press.

Easthope, Antony. 2013. *Poetry As Discourse*. New York, NY: Routledge. ProQuest EbookCentral, https://ebookcentralproquest.com.ezproxy3.library.arizona.edu/lib/UAZ/detail.action?docID=1517579.

Eliot, T.S. 1932. "The Metaphysical Poets." In *Selected Essays 1917–1932*. New York, NY: Harcourt, Brace and Company.

– 1998. *The Sacred Wood and Major Early Essays*. Mineola, NY: Dover.

Fisher, Tom. 2010. "Reading Renunciation: Laura Riding's Modernism and the End of Poetry." *Journal of Modern Literature* 33, no. 3: 1–19.

Foucault, Michel. 1970. *The Order of Things: An Archaeology of the Human Sciences*. Translated by Alan Sheridan. New York, NY: Vintage Books.

Grossman, Allen. 1992. *The Sighted Singer: Two Works on Poetry for Readers and Writers*. Baltimore and London: Johns Hopkins University Press.

Harney, Stefano, and Fred Moten. 2013. *The Undercommons: Fugitive Planning and Black Study*. London, UK: Minor Compositions.

Heidegger, Martin. 1962. *Being and Time*. Translated by John Macquarrie and Edward Robinson. New York, NY and London, UK: Harper Perennial.

– 1977. *The Question Concerning Technology and Other Essays*. Translated by William Lovitt. New York, NY and London, UK: Harper Perennial.

Heller-Roazen, Daniel. 2017. *No One's Ways: An Essay on Infinite Naming*. New York, NY: Zone Books.

Hjorth, Ben. 2014. "We're Standing in/the Nick of Time." Review in *Performance Research* 19, vol. 3: 135–9.

Hoberman, Mara. 2012. "Critic's Pick: Amy Sillman and Lisa Robertson." Review in *Artforum*, 25 June.

Hobson, Marian. 1998. *Jacques Derrida: Opening Lines*. New York, NY: Routledge.

Huddleston, Robert. 2015. "'Poetry Makes Nothing Happen': W.H. Auden's Struggle with Politics." *Boston Review*, 25 February 2015, http://bostonreview.net/poetry/robert-huddleston-wh-auden-struggle-politics.

Huizinga, Johan. 2014. *Homo Ludens: A Study of the Play Element in Culture*. Mansfield Centre, CT: Martino Publishing.

Jakobson, Roman. 1960. "Linguistics and Poetics." In *Style in Language*, edited by Thomas Albert Sebeok. Cambridge, MA: MIT Press.

Johnson, Barbara. 1986. "Apostrophe, Animation, and Abortion." *Diacritics* 16, no. 1 (Spring): 28–47.

Kafka, Franz. 1998. *The Trial*. Translated by Breon Mitchell. New York, NY: Knopf Doubleday Publishing Group.

Kearney, Douglas. 2015. *Mess and Mess and*. Blacksburg, VA: Noemi Press.

Kermode, Frank. 2000. *The Sense of an Ending: Studies in the Theory of Fiction*. Oxford and London, UK: Oxford University Press.

Lerner, Ben. 2016. *The Hatred of Poetry*. New York, NY: Farrar, Strauss and Giroux.

Levinas, Emmanuel. 1969. *Totality and Infinity: An Essay on Exteriority*. Translated by Alphonso Lingis. Pittsburgh, PA: Duquesne University Press.

Mallarmé, Stéphane. 2007. *Divagations*. Translated by Barbara Johnson. Cambridge, MA and London, UK: Belknap Press of Harvard University Press.

– 2011. *Collected Poems of Stéphane Mallarmé: A Bilingual Edition*. Berkeley, CA: University of California Press. ProQuest Ebook Central.

Meillassoux, Quentin. 2012. *After Finitude: An Essay on the*

Necessity of Contingency. Translated by Ray Brassier. New York, NY and London, UK: Continuum.

– 2012. *The Number and the Siren: A Decipherment of Mallarmé's* Coup de Dés. Translated by Robin Mackay. New York, NY: Sequence Press.

Moore, Marianne. 2017. *New Collected Poems*. Edited by Heather Cass White. New York, NY: Farrar, Straus and Giroux.

Moten, Fred. 2015. Cover endorsement for *Mess And Mess And*, by Douglas Kearney. Blacksburg, VA: Noemi Press.

Moure, Erín. 2008. *O Cidadán*. Toronto, ON: House of Anansi.

– 2012. *The Unmemntioable*. Toronto, ON: House of Anansi.

North, Michael. 2013. "The Making of 'Make It New.'" *Guernica Magazine*, 15 August 2013. https://www.guernicamag.com/the-making-of-making-it-new/.

OED Online. https://www.oed.com/. Accessed 21 April 2018.

O'Rourke, Megan. 2010. "The Unfolding: Anne Carson's *Nox*." Review of *Nox*, by Anne Carson. *New Yorker*, 12 July 2010. https://www.newyorker.com/magazine/2010/07/12/the-unfolding.

Oxford Annotated Bible. 1962. New York: Oxford University Press.

Paterson, Katie. "The Future Library." https://www.futurelibrary.no/#/the-artwork. Accessed 30 April 2018.

Philip, M. NourbeSe. 2008. *Zong!* Middletown, CT: Wesleyan University Press.

Plato. *The Republic.* Translated by Benjamin Jowett. Third edition, 1888. Oxford, UK: Clarendon Press.

Pound, Ezra. 1934. *ABC of Reading.* New York, NY: New Directions.

Prins, Y. 2015. "This Bird That Never Settles: A Virtual Conversation with Anne Carson about Greek Tragedy." *The Oxford Handbook of Greek Drama in the Americas.* Oxford, UK: Oxford University Press. ProQuest Ebrary.

Rawlings, Angela. 2015. "Ecolinguistic Activism and How to Rite." *Narrating Life: Immunity, Mutation, and Contagion.* Amsterdam: Rodopi/Brill.

– 2018. "The Importance of Oceanic Editors: An Interview with Angela Rawlings." *EuropeNow*, 17 April 2018.

Robertson, Lisa. 2009. *Magenta Soul Whip.* Toronto, ON: Coach House Books.

Rotman, Brian. 1978. *Signifying Nothing: The Semiotics of Zero.* Stanford, CA: Stanford University Press.

Rukeyser, Muriel. 1996. *The Life of Poetry.* Middletown, CT: Paris Press.

– 2005. *The Collected Poems of Muriel Rukeyser.* Edited by Janet E. Kaufman and Anne F. Herzog. Pittsburgh, PA: University of Pittsburgh Press.

Santos Perez, Craig. 2008. *Hacha.* Kaneohe, HI: Tinfish Press.

– 2010. *Saina.* Oakland, CA: Omnidawn Press.

– 2014. *Guma.* Oakland, CA: Omnidawn Press.

Sartre, Jean Paul. 1988. *"What Is Literature?" and Other Essays.* Translated by Bernard Frechtman. Cambridge, MA: Harvard University Press.

Savoy, Eric. 2017. "Between As If and Is: On Shirley Jackson." *Women's Studies* 46, no. 8: 827–44.

Schuster, Joshua. 2016. "On Reading Christian Bök's 'The Xenotext: Book 1' Ten Thousand Years Later: A Xeno-review." *Jacket2*, 17 February 2016. http://jacket2.org/reviews/reading-christian-boks-xenotext-book-1-ten-thousand-years-later.

Sedgwick, Eve Kosofsky. 2003. *Touching Feeling*. Durham, NC: Duke University Press.

Solnit, Rebecca. 2016. *Hope in the Dark: Untold Histories, Wild Possibilities*. New York, NY: Haymarket Books.

Steiner, George. 2012. "Anne Carson 'Translates' *Antigone*." Review of *Antigonick,* by Anne Carson. *Times Literary Supplement,* 1 August 2012. https://www.the-tls.co.uk/articles/public/anne-carson-translates-antigone/.

Stevens, Wallace. 1966. *Collected Poetry and Prose*. New York, NY: The Library of America.

Suicidegirls. 2012. "Anne Carson: Antigonick." Review. Suicidegirls.com, 29 July 2012. https://www.suicidegirls.com/girls/sash/blog/2680448/anne-carson-antigonick/.

Terada, Rei. 2009. *Phenomenality and Dissatisfaction, Kant to Adorno*. Cambridge, MA and London, UK: Harvard University Press.

Vaihinger, Hans. 1935. *The Philosophy of 'As If': A System of the Theoretical, Practical and Religious Fictions of Mankind*. Translated by C.K. Ogden. London, UK: Routledge and Kegan Paul Ltd.

Vicuña, Cecelia. 2012. *Spit Temple*. Translated by Rosa Alcala. Brooklyn, NY: Ugly Duckling Presse.

Voyce, Stephen. 2007. "The Xenotext Experiment: An Interview with Christian Bök." Toronto, ON: York University. http://pmc.iath.virginia.edu/issue.107/17.2voyce.html.

Woolf, Virginia. 1925. *The Common Reader*. San Diego, CA and New York, NY: Harcourt Brace Jovanovich.

Wynter, Sylvia. 2003. "Unsettling the Coloniality of Being/Power/Truth/Freedom towards the Human, After Man, Its Overrepresentation – An Argument." *New Centennial Review* 3, no. 3 (Fall 2003): 257–337.

Index

address, 6–7, 12, 25, 31–2, 37, 50, 83–5, 94, 98, 117, 122, 145, 147, 149, 152, 156
Adorno, Theodor, 19, 133
Agamben, Giorgio, 8, 44–5, 47–8
ambiguity, 14, 34, 45, 119, 124, 130, 133, 136, 156, 158
Aristotle, 14, 38, 119–21, 124, 133, 159

Badiou, Alain, 56, 150, 159, 163, 168
Bergson, Henri, 81–2, 85–6, 88, 94

Carson, Anne, 13, 60, 64, 96–118, 140, 164, 166
chance, 20, 52, 56–8, 72, 74, 140, 164. *See also* contingency
Christensen, Inger, 12, 18, 56, 58–68, 72, 78
Cixous, Hélène, 4–5, 9, 30, 132, 140–1, 161, 166
Coleridge, Samuel, 19, 157
colonialism, poetic approaches to the history of, 47, 71, 77–8, 125, 163
contingency, 57–8
Culler, Jonathan, 7, 43, 145

difference, 20, 25, 30–1, 44, 65, 104, 110–12, 137, 158
documentary poetry, 11–12, 18, 51, 70, 71, 77
dreams/dreaming, 28, 97–9, 101, 111, 161

edges, 13, 15, 67, 99, 102, 104–6, 109, 112, 166. *See also* embodiment; finitude; infinity; Levinas, Emmanuel
Eliot, T.S., 7, 157, 164
embodiment, 4–5, 14, 44, 70, 115, 126–7, 152. *See also* edges; finitude
enjambment, 6, 44–5, 122
ethics, 22, 31, 49–50, 52, 54, 77, 119–21, 133–4, 153. *See also* Aristotle; hope; Levinas, Emmanuel; poetic imperative

fact: as an expression or material reality or being, 10, 11, 18, 21, 25, 27, 29, 50, 107, 140, 143, 145, 158, 160; as distinguished from fiction, 26, 27, 41–4, 51, 158–9
failure, 19–20, 25, 69, 104, 126, 145. *See also* edges; finitude; hope; naming; unknown
fiction/fictionalism, 29, 30, 34. *See also* Vaihinger, Hans; Stevens, Wallace
finitude, 4, 9, 15, 26, 35, 43, 57, 67, 69, 72, 74, 78, 83–5, 127, 136, 149–50, 164. *See also* embodiment; enjambment; infinity
Foucault, Michel, 4, 155

grammar and/or punctuation, 22–4, 46, 58, 60–1, 63, 76, 123, 164

Heidegger, Martin, 8, 23, 83–4, 159, 161
hope, 4, 52, 54
human being: definition of, 3, 15, 37, 48; subjective experience of, 4, 9, 20–1, 32, 48–9, 54, 65–8, 97, 114–16, 119, 158. *See also* ambiguity; Linnaeus, Carl; paradox; *poiesis*

imagination, 24–6, 30, 62, 67, 72, 76, 111, 135, 139, 155, 165, 166
infinity: in relation to finitude, 4, 15, 67, 78, 83, 85, 125–6, 145; as an expression of what exceeds language and/or measure, 31, 35, 37, 43, 56–8, 74, 127, 131, 152, 156, 162. *See also* finitude; Other, the/Otherness
interpretation: in relation to poetic modes of reading, 29, 34, 36, 38, 88, 90, 103, 105, 109, 120, 121, 122, 124, 127, 128, 136, 138, 140, 143, 144, 146–7; in relation to the limits of subjective perception, 23, 26, 28, 39, 41, 58, 72, 74, 79, 84, 89, 106, 109, 115, 120, 122, 124, 133, 144, 151, 161; as a process of "making sense," 64, 94. *See also* Heidegger, Martin; imagination

joy, 53–4. *See also* Sedgwick, Eve; truth

Kafka, Franz, 98–9, 106
Kearney, Douglas, 14, 135–40
knowledge: pre-existing forms or limits of, 3, 6, 10, 16, 19, 29, 30, 46, 53, 54, 57, 63, 93, 104, 119, 130–2, 137, 138, 149, 153, 159; in relation to selfhood, language, and belief, 4, 5, 11, 26, 94, 98–101, 103, 109, 111, 144, 150, 152; in relation to truth, 10, 12, 21, 24, 31, 34, 41, 56, 81, 140, 149. *See also* fact; fiction/factionalism; human being; truth; unknown

Levinas, Emmanuel, 49, 125–6, 167
Linnaeus, Carl, 3, 36–7
lyric, 6–7, 43, 50, 151, 156–7. *See also* address

Mallarmé, Stephane, 11–12, 16–18, 56–8, 72, 77–8, 163–4
mathematics, 25, 26, 60–1, 80, 163. *See also* Badiou, Alain
Meillassoux, Quentin, 57–8, 150, 164
metaphor, 6, 25, 26, 28, 32, 34, 37, 121, 122, 124, 152
Modernism/Modernity, 6, 7, 10, 19, 83, 115, 151, 169. *See also* Stevens, Wallace
Moore, Marianne, 20, 160
Moten, Fred, 8, 135, 139

naming, 13, 21, 30, 36–7, 48, 58, 60, 70–1, 88, 98, 108, 117, 119, 123, 143, 169. *See also* limits; space

Other, the/Otherness, 4, 34, 44, 46, 49, 100, 144, 152, 167. *See also* Levinas, Emmanuel

paradox, 3, 9, 17, 44, 96–9, 101, 104, 107, 110–14, 116–17, 124, 126, 129. *See also* human being; Kafka, Franz
Perez, Craig Santos, 12, 18, 57, 70–8, 125, 140
poetic imperative, 4, 7, 14, 16, 17, 26, 54, 138. *See also* ethics; *poiesis*; self-reflexivity
poiesis, 8, 14, 29, 70, 83, 119–20, 133, 136, 159
politics, in relation to or in tension

with poetry, 8, 12, 17, 21–2, 55, 70–1, 76–8, 131–2, 134, 155, 157–9, 170
Pound, Ezra, 7, 89

Robertson, Lisa, 14, 128, 131–2, 136, 140

Sedgwick, Eve, 52–4, 124
self-reflexivity, 6, 8–9, 18, 37, 48, 50, 57, 78, 138, 149–52, 163. *See also* ethics
Solnit, Rebecca, 52, 54
space: in relation to an image or poetic text, 7, 68, 70, 72–4, 76, 81, 137; in relation to, or as produced through, poetic interpretation, 8, 10, 26, 31, 33, 48, 51–3, 56, 58, 66–7, 104, 106, 109, 112–13, 119, 130, 136, 144–5, 147, 162; in relation to time, 15, 77, 102, 142–3. *See also* edges; finitude
speculative, 5–6, 9–11, 24, 26, 144, 150. *See also* Badiou, Alain; Meillassoux, Quentin
Stevens, Wallace, 10, 23–35, 38–9, 152, 161, 165, 170

temporality, 8, 39, 42, 54, 58–9, 66, 68–9, 85, 116, 139, 144–6, 157–8; history/historical, 6, 8, 12–14, 21, 29, 47–8, 51–2, 55, 70–1, 75–7, 79–80, 83–4, 88–9, 93–5, 103, 109, 115–16, 120, 125, 132, 135, 137, 139–40, 143, 151, 156–7, 163, 169, future/futurity, 8, 12, 15, 29, 42, 52, 56, 58, 68–9, 73, 75, 90, 95, 142–8, 150, 152, 168; the present, 7–8, 12, 17, 20, 42, 49, 52, 58, 76, 81, 83, 88, 90, 103, 144–50, 155, 159, 160, 164
translation, 3, 11–14, 16, 18, 35, 41, 69, 72, 74, 83, 93, 100, 113–17, 121, 124, 142, 166, 168
truth: as an expression of, or in relation to subjective experience, interpretation and/or the imagination, 8, 19, 41, 51, 53, 105, 109, 119, 123, 125, 130, 137; as an expression of, or in relation to previously established categories of language and knowledge, 15, 17, 50–4, 124, 141; as an expression of, or in relation to the extralinguistic and/or the unknown, 4–5, 8–11, 18, 30, 41, 50, 58, 89, 101, 108–9, 114, 117, 131–2, 136, 140, 159, 161, 164. *See also* ambiguity; documentary poetry; imagination; *poiesis*

unknown: in relation to knowledge or the known, 4–6, 18, 76, 105, 147; as an expression of what exists beyond established categories, including language and selfhood, 7, 9, 28–9, 31, 35, 37, 42, 48, 52–4, 69, 74, 91, 98, 101, 117, 131, 135, 142, 144, 145–7, 149, 150–3, 156. *See also* hope; truth

Vaihinger, Hans, 29–30, 161

Woolf, Virginia, 5, 115, 156